SO-AZA-418

Ariel SHARON

Biography

Ariel SHARON

Norman H. Finkelstein

Lerner Publications Company
Minneapolis

For Tova and Joseph

WEBSITES
Website addresses in this book were valid at the time of printing. However, because of the nature of the Internet, some addresses may have changd or sites may have closed since publication. While the author and publisher regret any inconvenience this may cause readers, no responsibility for any such changes can be accepted by the author or publisher.

A&E and **BIOGRAPHY** are trademarks of A&E Television Networks. All rights reserved.

Some of the people profiled in this series have also been featured in the acclaimed BIOGRAPHY® series, on A&E Network, which is available on videocassette from A&E Home Video.

Copyright © 2005 by Norman H. Finkelstein

All rights reserved. International copyright secured. No part of this book may be reproduced, stored in a retrieval system, or transmitted in any form or by any means—electronic, mechanical, photocopying, recording, or otherwise—without the prior written permission of Lerner Publications Company, except for the inclusion of brief quotations in an acknowledged review.

This book is available in two editions:
Library binding by Lerner Publications Company,
a division of Lerner Publishing Group
Soft cover by First Avenue Editions,
an imprint of Lerner Publishing Group
241 First Avenue North
Minneapolis, MN 55401 U.S.A.

Website address: www.lernerbooks.com

Library of Congress Cataloging-in-Publication Data

Finkelstein, Norman H.
    Ariel Sharon / by Norman H. Finkelstein.
       p.   cm. — (A&E biography)
    Includes bibliographical references and index.
    ISBN: 0-8225-2370-1 (lib. bdg. : alk. paper)
    ISBN: 0-8225-9523-0 (pbk. : alk. paper)
    1. Sharon, Ariel. 2. Generals—Israel—Biography. 3. Prime
ministers—Israel—Biography. 4. Israel—History, Military. I. Title.
    II. Series.
DS126.6.S42F56   2005
956.9405'4—dc22   2004004701

Manufactured in the United States of America
1 2 3 4 5 6 – JR – 10 09 08 07 06 05

CONTENTS

An armed soldier of the Haganah (Israeli defenders) guards a secret road used to bring supplies to Jerusalem when Arab forces blockaded the city in 1948.

Chapter **ONE**

UNDER FIRE

THE ANCIENT AND HOLY CITY OF JERUSALEM IS important to both Jews and Arabs. Two thousand years ago, the Temple Mount in Jerusalem was the site of King Solomon's Temple, Judaism's holiest site. Temple Mount also holds two Muslim holy places, the Dome of the Rock and the al-Aqsa Mosque. When Israel declared its independence in 1948, the neighboring Arab states attacked the new nation. Jerusalem was the center of intense fighting between the Arabs and the Israelis. To force Jews out of the city, local Arab forces blocked key roads in early April 1948. They hoped to prevent food and supplies from reaching an increasingly besieged Jewish population. Arab troops from Jordan also moved in to block the road.

A key spot on the highway was the high ground at Latrun, capped by an imposing stone building that formerly served as a British police station.

Ariel Scheinerman, known by his friends as Arik, was a twenty-year-old platoon leader in the newly created Alexandroni Brigade of the Israeli army. When the brigade was given the order to retake Latrun, Arik's platoon joined in the attack. Many of the young platoon leader's soldiers were recent arrivals, untrained survivors of the Holocaust—Adolf Hitler's plan to exterminate the Jewish people in Europe during World War II (1939–1945). The attack was planned for the cover of darkness, but because of miscommunications, it began only at first light. The fighting was fierce. As artillery shells exploded around them and machine-gun fire kept them close to the ground, Arik's platoon was caught in an open field. Advance was impossible. Around them, other platoons had pulled back, and soon Arik's men were alone.

One soldier asked, "Arik, how are you going to get us out of this?"

"Look," he answered, "I've gotten you out of a lot of tight places before. I'll get you out of this too. Just get back and do what I told you."

The casualties mounted. Around him men were dead or wounded. As Arik raised himself slightly to get a better look at the scene, he, too, was hit. "I felt something thud into my belly, knocking me back." Bleeding and losing strength, Arik suddenly realized that the firing

Haganah members hold Castel Heights overlooking an important road linking Jerusalem to the Mediterranean Sea. During the Israeli War of Independence (1948), Sharon and other Israeli forces fought to capture such highlands and to control key roads.

had stopped. The silence was eerie. Looking beyond his position, he saw that the soldiers in other Israeli platoons had either withdrawn or were dead or dying.

The sight of Arab fighters slowly making their way down the hill spurred Arik to action. Most of his platoon was dead too. The remaining soldiers were wounded. He ordered those who could move to retreat. Those who could not move were left behind. Bleeding and in pain, he began to crawl away over the rough rocks.

A young member of his platoon who had been shot in the jaw crawled up to him, and together they supported each other to safety. The bitter memory of that battle never left young Arik Scheinerman, and it shaped the person he became—Ariel Sharon.

Like the people shown in this photograph, Ariel Sharon's parents emigrated from Europe to Palestine—an area of the Middle East near the Mediterranean Sea—in the 1920s.

Chapter **TWO**

BEGINNINGS OF
A SOLDIER

ARIEL SCHEINERMAN WAS BORN ON FEBRUARY 27, 1928, in Kfar Malal, a small, dusty, farming settlement. It is located fifteen miles north of Tel Aviv, a city in the modern State of Israel. His parents, Samuil and Dvora, had come here in 1922 from Russia. They were not alone. Along with thousands of other young idealistic Jews, they had moved to their ancient homeland to escape decades of religious and political discrimination in Eastern Europe and to build a new Jewish state there. Since the early 1880s, many waves of immigration had increased the Jewish population of Palestine. These waves were called Aliyot (singular Aliya), from the Hebrew word meaning "going up." The third Aliya, from 1919 to 1923, brought thirty-five thousand Jews to Palestine including Ariel's parents.

These settlers were dedicated Zionists, followers of Theodor Herzl's Zionist movement, which called for the establishment of a Jewish state. Samuil's father had been a delegate to the First Zionist Congress in Basel, Switzerland, in 1897, where political Zionism was born. From him, Samuil inherited a deep commitment to Zionism, a fervor passed down to his son Ariel.

Life in the Yishuv—the Jewish settlement in Palestine —was harsh and dangerous. The tiny settlement in which the Scheinermans lived had no electricity. The quality of the farmhouses depended on the building skills of their owners. The Scheinerman house was roughly put together with large gaps between the wallboards. Frequent raids by unwelcoming Arab neighbors added to the tension. Yet no matter how difficult the living conditions, the residents were committed to maintaining a foothold in the Jewish homeland.

Like their other Jewish neighbors, the Scheinermans were tough and resilient. But unlike most of their neighbors, who were dedicated to community cooperation, the Scheinermans were aloof and controversial. They considered themselves intellectuals, superior to the other settlers in Kfar Malal. Samuil, his son later said, "was by nature unable to compromise nor was he the kind to keep his mouth shut . . . if he thought something was wrong, he came out and said it. And if he was convinced of his position, he would not give in."

THE ZIONIST DREAM

fter the destruction of the Holy Temple in Jerusalem by the Romans in A.D. 70, nearly all Jews dispersed to other lands. After the Jews had left, their homeland, which they called Israel, was settled by Arab tribes. Still there had always been a small number of Jews in Palestine. Jews, unable to return to their ancient homeland ruled by others, never forgot Jerusalem in their hearts and prayers wherever they went. One traditional Jewish ceremony ends with the words "Next year in Jerusalem."

For nearly two thousand years after Jews were exiled from Israel, they lived in countries far and wide. They were persecuted and discriminated against in these countries too. At the First Zionist Congress in Basel, Switzerland, in 1897, Dr. Theodor Herzl established the political and organizational structure that led to the founding of the modern State of Israel. He began his diplomatic negotiations with world powers and created a Zionist leadership organization. Herzl gained international support for Zionism, the return of the Jewish people to their ancient homeland in the Middle East.

Writing in his diary after the Zionist Congress in 1897, Herzl, who died in 1904, asserted, "At Basel I founded the Jewish State. If I said this out loud today, I would be answered by universal laughter. Perhaps in five years, and certainly in fifty, everyone will know it."

Both parents were devoted to Ariel, who was called Arik, and to his older sister Dita. Yet Ariel recalled, "My father, Samuil and my mother, Vera, were a different sort of people, not given to displaying their feelings, no matter how strong these might have been . . . they did not wear their hearts on their sleeves. What my parents did exude was strength, determination, and stubbornness." These were the same characteristics that would later define Arik Sharon.

The British had assumed rule of much of the Middle East, including Palestine, following World War I (1914–1918). In 1917 the British government issued the Balfour Declaration, named for Lord Balfour, the British prime minister. It announced support for "the establishment in Palestine of a national home for the Jewish people." But Britain was unable or unwilling to protect Jews from their Arab neighbors during riots in 1920 and 1921. The constant tension with Arabs affected Yishuv life. Local Jewish defense groups collectively known as the Haganah (the defenders) informally organized themselves to protect their communities.

In August 1929, a series of particularly violent riots by Arabs took the lives of hundreds of Jews throughout Palestine. As a result of the riots of 1929, the Haganah transformed itself into an unofficial military that included nearly all men in rural villages and a large number from the cities. They trained officers and soldiers and began to import and secretly store small

arms. Their mission was twofold: first, to protect
Yishuv Jews from Arab attacks; and second, to prepare
for the eventual establishment of a Jewish state.

From early childhood, Arik worked on the farm. He
helped his parents in their fields with jobs that
included clearing rocks and plowing. As he grew older,
he did night duty, guarding his family's crops from
thieves with a fancy dagger given to him by his father.
Because of the family's independence and criticism of
their neighbors, others in the community shunned the
Scheinermans and Arik had few friends.

Arik's parents wanted more for their son. They regis-
tered him in a prestigious high school in Tel Aviv, an
hour's commute away.

"For me," Arik said, "Tel Aviv was a godsend." His
daily trips to the major city of Jewish Palestine
opened his eyes to a world beyond his rural farming
community. He was an eager student, and he found
friends to whom he could easily relate.

But neither the village of Kfar Malal nor the city of
Tel Aviv were immune from the news coming out of
Europe. The Nazi leadership in Germany seemed
unstoppable as their armies overran most of Europe
during World War II. Of deep concern to many in the
Yishuv was the fate of relatives and friends in Europe.
Jewish paramilitary groups including the Haganah
temporarily put aside their arguments with the British
to join them in the fight against the Nazis. At the age
of fourteen, Arik was accepted into the Haganah.

He "stood in front of a Bible and a pistol and took an oath of allegiance." On Saturdays and evenings, after his long trip home from Tel Aviv, Arik joined other young people from Kfar Malal in military training. They were getting ready for the time a Jewish state would finally be established in Palestine.

Life for Arik was not all school, military drills, and farmwork. One day while out in his family's field, he noticed a particularly pretty girl in the school next door. After days of considering how to go about meeting her, he took a direct route by cutting the fence between the two properties. The girl, Margalit (Gali) Zimmerman, was a sixteen-year-old from Romania who had escaped the Nazis. Gali and Arik became close friends, perhaps the only real friend Arik had made in Kfar Malal.

In 1945, at the age of seventeen, Arik, along with the other Jews in Palestine, celebrated the end of World War II. The global war was over and the Nazis defeated, but the fight to create a Jewish state was only beginning. Following the horrors of the Holocaust, the dream of establishing an independent Jewish nation in Palestine seemed to be coming true. The world, perhaps feeling some responsibility for the deaths of six million Jews by the Nazis, sympathized with the plight of desperate Jewish survivors. Hundreds of thousands of war refugees were living in primitive camps throughout Europe. They had no homes they could return to. (To avoid conflict with Arab nations during World War II, Britain halted all

Jewish immigration to Palestine in 1944.) After the war, pressure mounted on Great Britain to lift the strict immigration rules for Palestine and admit large numbers of Jews.

There was much at stake. For Arabs it meant sharing the single small land of Palestine with Jews. For Jews it meant the fulfillment of the two-thousand-year dream of returning to the home of their ancestors. While diplomats discussed the problem, a highly organized large-scale movement began to bring Jewish survivors of the Holocaust to Palestine illegally. Violence against British troops increased, while Arab attacks on Jews grew in number and intensity. By 1947 the British, seeing no end to the growing violence, turned the Palestine problem over to the newly formed international peace-keeping organization called the United Nations (UN). Furious debate began at the United Nations on a partition plan to divide Palestine into separate nations, one Jewish and one Arab.

Arik's father wanted him to continue his education after high school by studying agriculture at a nearby branch of the Hebrew University. But Arik had other ideas. With the future of a Jewish state finally becoming a reality, yet threatened with destruction by Arab forces, Arik joined the Haganah infantry.

Concerned with mounting Arab attacks on isolated Jewish settlements, the British created the Jewish Settlement Police Force and recruited young Jewish men. The training was professional and provided a legal way for Haganah members to prepare for the battles to come. For most of 1947, Arik faced nearly daily actions against Arab forces. The young man who had grown up lonely and shy quickly gained confidence in himself and became a leader.

On November 29, 1947, the General Assembly of the United Nations voted for the partition of Palestine. The vote created an independent Jewish state in Palestine for the first time in two thousand years. The plan called for the division of Jerusalem. The western part would be Israeli. The eastern part, including the Old City and Temple Mount, was to be under Jordanian control.

In spite of this loss of their ancient holy sites, the Jews favored the plan. Nearly all Arabs were united against it. Even as diplomacy was ongoing, Arab troops attacked Jewish targets in Palestine. A main aim was to control major roads and to isolate the scattered Yishuv settlements. The U.S. ambassador to the United Nations predicted that once the British left, the combined armies of five neighboring Arab countries—Egypt, Syria, Lebanon, Jordan, and Iraq—would sweep into Palestine and "drive the Jews into the sea."

On May 14, 1948, as the combined Arab armies encircled the settlements, David Ben-Gurion, Israel's first prime minister, proclaimed the creation of the State of Israel. Soon after, the Yishuv's previously illegal, armed defense groups combined into the young country's official military organization, the Israel Defense Forces (IDF). One day later, Arab armies attacked the Jewish

Standing below a portrait of Zionist Theodor Herzl, Israeli prime minister David Ben-Gurion, center, *announces the establishment of the independent State of Israel in Tel Aviv on May 14, 1948.*

nation from all sides. The war for Israel's independence was on.

Hundreds of thousands of Arab residents of Palestine fled the fighting by crossing into neighboring Arab lands, hoping to return once the Jews were defeated. Arik led his platoon of soldiers in a failed attempt to stop the Arab advance on the Latrun outpost. It was there he suffered his first wounds of battle.

Many Palestinians, such as this woman and child, became refugees when they fled the fighting in Palestine during the 1948 war for Israel's independence.

In the hospital, Arik had many visitors to cheer him during his recuperation, including Gali, whom he had frequently visited between Haganah missions. But he found his thoughts returning to the men who had died. Many of the recruits went into the army directly from the ships that brought them to Israel. Many others were the sons of neighbors at Kfar Malal and the other settlements Arik knew so well. The hospital stay gave Arik time to think about what had happened. "At the age of twenty," he later wrote, "twenty of my best friends were dead.

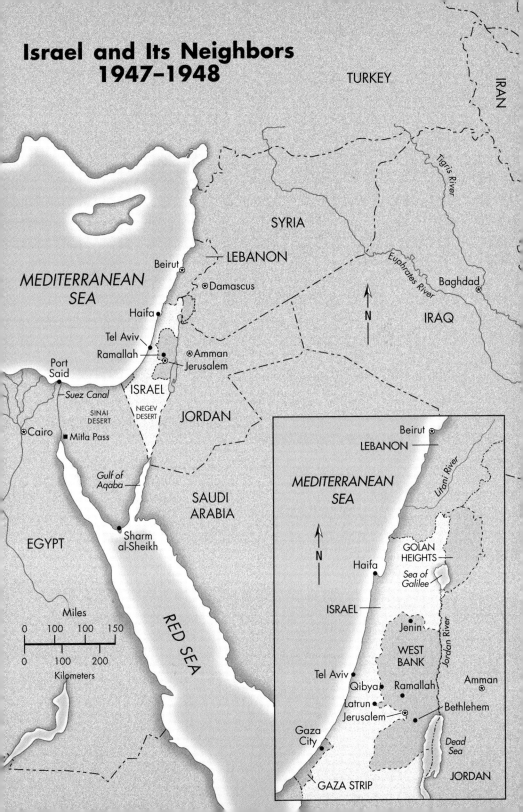

Israel and Its Neighbors
1947–1948

TURKEY

IRAN

SYRIA

LEBANON

Beirut ⊛

⊛ Damascus

Tigris River

Euphrates River

Baghdad ⊛

MEDITERRANEAN
SEA

Haifa ●

Tel Aviv ●

Ramallah ●

⊛ Amman
Jerusalem

N

IRAQ

Port
Said

Suez Canal

ISRAEL

NEGEV
DESERT

JORDAN

SINAI
DESERT

⊛ Cairo ■ Mitla Pass

Gulf of
Aqaba

SAUDI
ARABIA

EGYPT

Sharm
al-Sheikh ●

Miles

0   100   100   150

0   100   200

Kilometers

RED SEA

MEDITERRANEAN
SEA

Beirut ⊛

LEBANON

Litani River

N

GOLAN
HEIGHTS

Haifa ●

Sea of
Galilee

ISRAEL

Jordan River

Jenin ●

WEST
BANK

Tel Aviv ●

Qibya ●

Ramallah ●

Amman ⊛

Latrun ●

Bethlehem ●

Jerusalem ⊛

Gaza
City ●

Dead
Sea

GAZA STRIP

JORDAN

I had participated in a number of daring small-scale victories but I had also been involved in some of the army's most dreadful failures." He questioned the planning and execution of the failed Latrun attack. Over and over in his mind, he questioned why higher-ranking officers were not present to coordinate the attack.

Years later, he remarked, "I remember that as I lay in the hospital, I was eaten up by the despair and shame of the defeat. I had thought I would not continue to serve in the army. For like many others, I had enlisted in order to end the war as soon as possible and go home. I had plans of going on to study agriculture like my father and work on the farm. But that awful feeling of helplessness was too terrible to forget."

Arik returned to his unit convinced that "one of the foremost duties of a soldier is the duty of saving a fellow fighter at all costs, even at the threat to his personal safety." This belief was later adopted by the Israeli military as an unwritten rule.

Arik became an intelligence officer for the Golani Brigade after his old Alexandroni Brigade was moved to reserve (noncombat) status. For the next couple of years, he gathered information, trained recruits, and continued to engage in night skirmishes with Egyptian and Jordanian soldiers who were constantly sneaking into Israel. His diligence and leadership were recognized. In 1950 he was appointed a captain and assigned as an intelligence officer, first for the army's Central Command and soon after for the Northern Command.

In 1952 Arik took a two-month leave of absence from the army to recover from a bout of malaria. During his leave, he especially enjoyed touring and exploring the American South.

When he returned refreshed and renewed at the end of 1952, he decided it was time for him to direct his own life. On March 29, 1953, he married Margalit and settled down as a newlywed undergraduate student at Hebrew University in Jerusalem. There he studied Middle Eastern history.

This was a dangerous period for Israelis. The Arab nations refused to accept the fact that Israel existed as a nation, so postwar skirmishes dragged on. Arab soldiers constantly crossed Israel's borders to kill Jewish residents and destroy their property. Between 1949 and 1953, many Jews—mainly civilians—were killed by Arab civilians in undercover guerrilla attacks and many more were wounded. Damage to agricultural and construction equipment mounted. Travel became dangerous, and residents of isolated settlements feared for their lives. In response to these raids, Israel's army attacked targets in Jordan and Egypt. Yet for all its training, the IDF was unable to stop the attacks. The nighttime raids by Israeli soldiers into Arab territory were often unsuccessful. It was not long before Arik was again called to serve his country.

Israeli soldiers learn commando (attack) skills near Haifa, Israel, during the 1950s. Israel's first commandos were unofficial fighters. Sharon was among them.

Chapter **THREE**

COMMANDO UNIT 101

IN JUNE 1953, ARIK WAS SUMMONED TO MILITARY headquarters. Although he was a university student, he, like most other Israelis not on active army duty, trained part-time with the army reserves. A particularly vicious Arab chief and his men had lately been crossing over the border into Israel almost nightly. The result was a growing number of dead Israelis.

Arik was asked to put together an unofficial group to go into Jordanian territory to blow up the chief's home in the village of Nebi Samuel. Arik called on a few other former soldiers. Dressed in civilian clothes, they crossed the border under cover of darkness and made their way to the village. The attack was not totally successful. The intruders lost the element of surprise by arriving noisily just as light dawned, and some of their explosives did not go off as planned. Arik returned to headquarters angry and disappointed. He told his superior officer that the raid was amateurish. What was needed, Arik firmly announced, was a fully trained and organized commando unit.

Arik's suggestion for a trained commando unit was passed up the chain of command to General Moshe Dayan, then the army's head of operations. Dayan recalled, "We were in need of a man of daring, a man with a great deal of personal ambition, a skilled leader, who would be flexible and original enough to adapt literal orders according to the situation he found himself in." That man, Dayan and Prime Minister David Ben-Gurion decided, was Ariel Scheinerman. By the end of July, Arik had reluctantly left the university and was ordered to organize a special army group, Commando Unit 101, to combat terrorism.

Ben-Gurion "saw in Arik the realization of the new Israeli." The prime minister was born and educated in Europe. To him, the young, opinionated, and decisive native-born Arik demonstrated a bravery and self-confidence often lacking in Jews who had grown up in Europe. Ben-Gurion (following a popular custom in the newly established Jewish state) even selected a Hebrew name for Ariel Scheinerman. He called him Ariel Sharon.

Commando Unit 101 was unlike any other group in the Israel Defense Forces. Sharon gathered together an

elite group of fifty daring soldiers. Each one was personally motivated to succeed. The atmosphere in their
training camp was casual and unmilitary. The goal was
to achieve perfection in physical conditioning and tac-
tical training. Yet the men were free to develop and
share their own ideas and to experiment with a variety
of techniques. They practiced continually under the
most realistic conditions. Nightly infiltrations across
the Jordanian border increased their self-confidence.
The men quickly learned from their mistakes and,
most important, learned to work as a group.

Their mission was to hit back at terrorists, to convey
the strong message that no attack on Israelis would go
unpunished. "I came to believe," Sharon later said,
"that whenever we were forced to strike, we should do
so with the aim of inflicting heavy losses on enemy
troops . . . to neutralize the Arab's desire to make war
on us . . . to convince the Arabs that war was futile,
that aggression would bring them nothing but humili-
ation and destruction."

The commandos of Unit 101 often did not distinguish
between military and civilian targets. Israel was frequently criticized by other countries for excessively
punishing innocent people. In spite of Sharon's tough
military actions and reliance on careful planning and
training, Unit 101 could do little to stop the continual
Arab attacks. Yet the actions of Unit 101 were popular
with Israelis. That same training later became a stan-
dard for all the Israel Defense Forces.

On the evening of October 12, 1953, Arabs crossed the Jordanian border and entered the Israeli settlement of Moshav Yahud. A hand grenade thrown into a house caused the deaths of two small children and their mother. Two days later, Sharon, leading his own Unit 101 and a brigade of paratroopers (soldiers who jump from aircraft into battle), crossed into Jordan and entered the village of Qibya, where they believed guerrilla activity was centered. "Qibya," Sharon later wrote, "was to be a lesson." His orders were to inflict heavy casualties on Jordanian soldiers as a message that "Jewish blood could no longer be shed."

The soldiers ordered residents to leave their homes. As people fled, the troops placed explosives around homes they believed to be empty of people and destroyed more than forty buildings. Sharon and his men returned to their base satisfied that they had accomplished what they set out to do. The next day, they and the world were shocked to learn that more than fifty civilians, hiding in the houses, died when the buildings were blown up. The world was outraged.

The United States immediately denounced the attack. At the UN, Israel was condemned and officially reprimanded by the UN Security Council, which refused to condemn Arab terrorist attacks. Abba Eban, Israel's ambassador to the United States, defended Israel. "The whole of Israel is a frontier. The Arab governments refuse to live in peace with Israel; and they also refuse to let Israel live in peace." His words fell on deaf ears.

General Moshe Dayan, left, *meets with Major Ariel Sharon during the 1950s. Dayan, chief of the Israeli army's general staff, selected Sharon to command the para-commando Unit 202.*

In December 1953, Moshe Dayan was appointed chief of the army's general staff. One of his first decisions was to combine Commando Unit 101 with the paratroop brigade. He promoted Ariel Sharon to major and gave him command over the reorganized combat team. The paratroopers were suspicious of the unmilitary manners of the commandos, and the commandos did not welcome the military strictness. Nonetheless, Sharon managed to bring the two different styles into a single cohesive group. Border attacks increased, and Sharon's new command, called Unit 202, was kept busy fighting.

One result of the Qibya action was an order prohibiting future direct attacks on women and children.

From 1954 to 1956, Sharon organized and led over seventy raids on military targets. He taught his officers to always lead their troops into battle. For him, that was not just a rule but a way of life. Danger was always lurking, and on one attack on an Egyptian position, Sharon was wounded again.

In February 1955, an Israeli worker was killed near Gaza, a strip of land along the Mediterranean between Egypt and Israel that was controlled by Egypt. Sharon led his paratroopers on a daring retaliatory raid, targeting the main Egyptian army base deep in Gaza. The mission was accomplished with a great loss of Egyptian life and weaponry but also many Israeli casualties. The United Nations quickly censured Israel, but again it failed to recognize the guerrilla actions by Arabs that had forced Israel's response. The attacks and reprisals continued unabated as the world just watched.

Egyptian leader Gamal Abdel Nasser, in power since 1952, was vehemently opposed to Israel's existence. In 1955 he allied himself with the Soviet Union. Eager to flex its muscles as a political force in the Middle East and compete with the United States, the Soviets began supplying Egypt with modern arms, tanks, and airplanes. Feeling increasingly confident, Nasser fanned the flames of war as other Arab countries joined in. "The time has come," a Jordanian military leader said, "when the Arabs will be able to choose the time for an offensive to liquidate Israel." Tensions were high.

With the United States refusing to become involved, Israel turned to Britain and France as a source for arms to keep up with the Egyptians.

While planning a reprisal raid on an Egyptian outpost in the Sinai Desert, Ariel Sharon also was in the midst of a court-martial trial. The quick-tempered Sharon was accused of slapping a soldier in 1954. The soldier had been a prisoner under arrest for escaping. The man had since committed suicide, but the case dragged on, keeping Sharon from concentrating on his work. Finally, Sharon asked General Dayan to interfere on his behalf. The charges were dropped.

Emboldened by support from the Soviet Union, Nasser massed Egyptian troops in the Sinai Desert, and by April he had begun preparations for an actual attack. He increased the tension by sponsoring terrorist attacks on Israeli civilian buses, homes, and oil and gas pipelines. Each succeeding Egyptian attack resulted in Israeli retaliation.

Egypt closed the Gulf of Aqaba to Israeli shipping. Jordan denied Jews of all countries access to Jewish holy places in East Jerusalem and the West Bank of the Jordan River, areas controlled by the Jordanians. In response to a particularly bloody attack from across the Jordanian border, Sharon led a raid on Jordanian police headquarters. Sharon shrugged off the casualties as "unavoidable" and correctly predicted that "we are seeing the end of the policy of reprisals." The next step was war.

The Suez Canal in Egypt, connecting the Mediterranean with the Red Sea, had opened in 1869. Owned
jointly by Britain and France, international law guar-
anteed safe passage to ships of all nations. But in
1948, the canal had been closed to Israeli shipping. In
1956 Nasser seized control of the Suez Canal from
Britain and France. The seizure angered both Britain
and France, and they entered into a secret agreement
with Israel to launch a surprise war against Egypt.
Victory would return control of the Suez Canal to the
Europeans and guarantee Israel's right of passage
through it. The 1956 Sinai War began on October 29
with a drop of Israeli paratroopers at the Mitla Pass
deep in the Sinai Desert. To the Egyptians, it looked
like just another Israeli reprisal raid. While battalions
took positions on the ground, Sharon and another
brigade moved quickly on land toward Mitla with
tanks and armored vehicles.

Although air reconnaissance reported no enemy
troops guarding the pass, Sharon requested permission several times to send a force through to ensure
that the area was secure. General Dayan, concerned
about bogging troops down in unnecessary fighting,
finally ordered Sharon to send only a small patrol to
scout the pass. If they engaged a larger enemy, they
were to withdraw. Sharon, true to his own independence and always ready for a good fight, sent in a
large combat team, which quickly came under wither-
ing fire. Egyptian troops were hidden in the many

Israeli soldiers receive congratulations from the Israeli government for their capture of the Egyptian fort at Sharm al-Sheikh on the Gulf of Aqaba in November 1956.

caves above the pass. The toll on the Egyptians was heavy, but nearly forty Israeli paratroopers were killed and many more wounded in the bloody ambush. Again Sharon was accused of ignoring orders.

The following week, on November 5, British and French forces landed in Port Said, at the entrance of the Suez Canal. The United States was surprised and furious. President Dwight Eisenhower turned to the United Nations, which ordered an immediate cease-fire and the withdrawal of British, French, and Israeli armed forces. Israel, in the short war, succeeded in capturing the entire Sinai Peninsula and retook access to the Gulf of Aqaba at the northern end of the Red Sea.

Israel finally withdrew from captured Egyptian territory only after assurances that UN troops would be
deployed to guarantee the rights of Israeli shipping
and prevent guerrilla incursions into Israel from Gaza.

Army leaders could not forget the Mitla Pass incident.
While they appreciated Sharon's skills, they did not like
his arrogance and cavalier attitude. Sharon was angry
that Israel had agreed to give up the territory it had
captured in exchange for UN guarantees of safety. He
believed that another war was inevitable. With the war
over, Ariel Sharon went home to Gali, who was expect-
ing their first child. On December 27, 1956, a son, Gur,
was born. The joy was tempered three days later when
Arik learned that his father had died.

In 1957 Ariel Sharon was sent to England to study
at the British army staff college. He learned to appre-
ciate all the formal traditions that were part of British
military life. They contrasted sharply with the harsh
and direct attitudes of his own army.

On his return to Israel, Sharon was promoted to
colonel and assigned to command infantry training.
To Sharon, the man of action and daring, this assignment was boring. But as a good soldier, he carried out
the rather easy assignment for four years. It also gave
him the opportunity to resume his studies.

Ever eager to improve his military skill, he also
enrolled in the army's armor school. After his experi-
ences in the Sinai, he believed that tanks would be the
difference between success and failure in future wars.

On May 2, 1962, sadness struck again. His wife Gali was killed in an automobile accident on her way to work as a psychiatric nurse. Ariel and son Gur, then five years old, were devastated. Lily, Gali's sister, came to live with the Sharons and care for Gur. Arik and Lily fell in love, and they were married in August 1963.

In that same year, the new army head, Yitzhak Rabin, appointed Sharon as chief of staff for the Northern Command, where, for several years, friction with the Lebanese and the Syrians had escalated into frequent violence. In August 1964, the Sharons' son Omri was born.

At the end of 1964, needing a change of scene, Arik requested a leave of absence, and he and an army friend traveled to several African countries. It surprised him to find so many Israelis working there to improve agriculture and health. Then he returned to the Northern Command to await what he thought was a long-deserved promotion and new assignment.

He waited nervously until finally summoned to Yitzhak Rabin's office. Rabin began by criticizing Sharon for his previous behavior and actions. Then, to Sharon's relief, Rabin promoted him to major general and appointed him director of military training. Sharon felt that preparing the military for a possible new war was an important contribution to his country's protection. Six months later, his third son, Gilad Yehuda, was born. Arik finally received his law degree from Hebrew University in 1966.

Israeli soldiers monitor Egyptian activity along the Suez Canal in 1967. The men are looking for advance signs of attack on Israel's border.

Chapter **FOUR**

THE SIX-DAY WAR

THE **1956** WAR IN THE SINAI HAD PROVIDED ISRAEL with important gains. It also taught the Israelis that they could not fully depend on others for protection. Relative calm had prevailed on Israel's borders in the years immediately following the war, but gradually, the occasional small-scale attacks increased in size, particularly from across the Syrian border. Even as tension along Israel's borders increased, the Soviet Union was involving itself more directly in Middle East affairs. Eager to influence the Arab world, the Soviets provided their Arab clients with the latest in arms and encouraged anti-Israel actions.

On April 7, 1967, Syrian troops fired at the driver of a lone Israeli tractor. Israel retaliated with an artillery duel that quickly escalated into an air battle. During this battle, the Israeli air force shot down six Syrian jet fighters. To stir up even more trouble, the Soviets accused Israel of moving large numbers of troops to the Syrian border. In spite of Israel's assurances that the charges were false, a war atmosphere quickly engulfed the region.

On May 16, Egypt requested the United Nations to immediately withdraw all troops of the UN Emergency Force stationed on Egyptian soil—in northern Sinai and at Sharm al-Sheikh at the gateway to the Gulf of Aqaba. To the astonishment of many, the United Nations immediately obliged. Gamel Abdel Nasser made no pretense about his plans. "Our basic objective," he said, "will be to destroy Israel."

The assurances of protection given by the UN, which had led Israel to withdraw from captured Sinai in 1956, were instantly dissolved. By early June, a combined Arab force of 250,000 soldiers, two thousand tanks, and seven hundred military aircraft from Egypt, Syria, and Jordan surrounded Israel. On May 22 Nasser again closed the Gulf of Aqaba to Israeli shipping, a blatant act of war. Israel felt vulnerable and isolated. When diplomatic efforts to diffuse the situation failed, Israel quietly mobilized its citizen army and made preparations for war. The outlook for survival was so grave that Israel's political parties joined in a national emergency government with General Moshe Dayan as the new defense minister.

Sharon went to the Negev Desert to prepare his reserve division for battle. He was concerned about the government's lack of specific goals for the impending war and was not shy in offering his opinion. "I told the prime minister that in my opinion the Israeli army could defeat the Egyptians utterly. I warned against going in phases." Sharon and other military leaders advised a quick and massive attack on the Egyptian forces.

On the morning of July 5, in a series of coordinated surprise attacks against Arab air bases, Israel virtually destroyed the combined air forces of Egypt, Jordan, and Syria and assumed complete superiority in the air. Israel sent a message to King Hussein of Jordan urging him to stay out of the war. Hussein, however, chose to believe the assurances of Nasser that Egyptian troops were already at the outskirts of Tel Aviv and sent Jordanian troops into action.

On the ground, Israeli troops quickly overran Egyptian positions in the Sinai Peninsula. The main objective was to reach the Suez Canal and the southern tip of the Sinai. The complex operation, which later was considered one of the world's classic military battles, was carried out at night with armored and infantry forces, helicopter paratroopers, and reserve forces.

Major General Ariel Sharon's armored division, in a carefully planned and executed attack, overtook the main Egyptian fortifications and reached the banks of the Suez Canal. Sharon's tanks, along with the other

Israeli units, forced the Egyptians to seek out the narrow Mitla Pass as their only escape route to the Suez Canal. The overwhelming Israeli air power hammered the defenseless vehicles into rubble.

Sharon found the scene "indescribable. The entire pass was choked with the wreckage of the Egyptian army. Tanks, artillery, half-tracks." The Egyptians had lost 80 percent of their entire army's military equipment. Sharon said, "Our soldiers are fantastic. In our army the word 'Forward!' practically doesn't exist— officers yell 'Follow me!' It's our secret weapon, the secret of our success, not the tanks and the artillery."

In the ninety-six hour war, Israel had regained all of the Sinai Peninsula given back to Egypt in 1956, the

Major General Ariel Sharon, left, in May 1967. His troops forced Egyptian army units into the Mitla Pass, where their tanks and artillery were reduced to scrap heaps by Israeli air strikes.

Egyptians flying Soviet-made MiG fighter planes attack the Israeli army as it advances toward the Suez Canal in June 1967. The Soviets chose to supply Arab forces during the war.

West Bank of the Jordan River ruled by Jordan since 1948, and the Golan Heights at the Syrian border. Perhaps the most momentous accomplishment was the Israeli capture of the entire city of Jerusalem. On June 7, Israeli paratroopers entered the Old City of Jerusalem and reclaimed the Western Wall of Solomon's Temple, under Jordanian rule since 1948.

All of Israel was elated and relieved at the war's successful outcome. Israel controlled three times as much land as before the war. The original hope was that this decisive victory would encourage the surrounding Arab nations to make peace with the Jewish state. Instead, the cycle of Arab violence intensified in spite of a cease-fire agreement brokered by the United States.

After the embarrassing defeat of the 1967 war and with the continued failure of the Arab nations to defeat Israel, many Palestinians, particularly those who still lived in the refugee camps, decided to take action on their own. The Palestinian refugees had been under Jordanian, Egyptian, and Syrian rule and did not have their own, separate nation. The Palestine Liberation Organization (PLO) had been organized in 1964 to work for an Arab Palestinian homeland. Under the leadership of Yasser Arafat, the PLO stepped up diplomatic and guerrilla activity against Israel.

With the war over, Sharon returned to his family. Like many other proud Israelis, he took his wife and oldest son to visit the holy sites that were open to them in Jerusalem. When he returned to work, he considered the problems Israel faced. The country controlled new land areas and the Arab populations that lived in them. Sharon felt that an Israeli military presence was necessary on the West Bank and set out to "establish Jewish footholds as fast as possible." As a first step, he planned to move a number of military training schools there.

Most Israelis hoped that the Arabs would finally realize that the Jewish state was not going away. Israel sent word to Egypt and Jordan that it would quickly return the captured territory in return for peace and for recognition of Israel as a nation. The response from the Arabs was quick and negative—no peace, no recognition, and no negotiation. The Soviet

Union provided Egypt with increasingly sophisticated weapons, including missiles. Soviet pilots began to fly missions for the Egyptians.

Tragedy again struck Sharon on the eve of Rosh Hashanah, the Jewish New Year, on October 4, 1967. He was alone at home on the telephone when he heard a gunshot outside. He opened the front door to find his twelve-year-old son, Gur, lying dead on the ground. Gur and his friends had been playing with one of Sharon's antique guns. When one of the friends accidentally loaded the gun and playfully aimed it at Gur, it went off. A tearful Sharon buried his son next to Margalit, the boy's mother. The Sharons were devastated.

Embarrassed by the overwhelming defeat in the 1967 war, the Egyptians began continual harassment across the Israeli border. Senior officers in the military wanted to reinforce the Israeli presence along the Suez Canal border with Egypt. A plan emerged to establish a series of forts connected by tunnels directly along the canal. This Bar-Lev Line, named after the head of Israel's army, required complicated engineering and construction.

Sharon vehemently objected to the plan. He even walked out of an important general staff meeting convened to discuss the issue. He had argued in vain against a permanent line of fortifications. The idea was an old one. The French had constructed their similar Maginot Line in World War II, and the Germans quickly overran it. Sharon instead called for mobile tank units stationed several miles apart on the Israeli side of the canal that could quickly respond to any Egyptian attempts to cross the water.

Sharon was not in step with the military leaders. His unpopularity and combative style delayed advancement of his army career, and he was bypassed for important assignments. Nonetheless, he continued to perform his training duties with diligence.

When his tour of duty ended in 1968, Sharon was astonished when General Bar-Lev refused his routine request to reenlist. Hurt and disappointed, Sharon considered his future. "I was at a dead end," he later said. "At the age of forty-one I was not exactly ready for pipe and slippers." Politics had always interested him, and this seemed like a perfect time to seek office. He met with the Likud Party leader, Menachem Begin, to seriously explore running for the Knesset, Israel's parliament, in the upcoming elections.

News of Sharon's interest in a political career caused leaders of the governing Labor Party and sympathetic military leaders to change their minds. Sharon was a well-known public figure, and he was well liked by the men who had served under him. He was sure to be popular in the voting booths. Grudgingly, General Bar-Lev approved Sharon's reenlistment. But to keep him away from military leadership, he was sent abroad on a public relations assignment.

In the spring of 1969, Egyptian leader Nasser declared a formal end to the cease-fire agreement of 1967, which he had never truly honored. With the assurance of continued aid from the Soviet Union, he escalated cross-border raids on Israeli targets. When U.S. secretary of state William Rogers stepped in to stop the violence, both Israel and Egypt agreed to reestablish the cease-fire. Egypt immediately broke the short-lived peace by moving Soviet-supplied surface-to-air missiles into the Suez Canal area.

Sharon received orders to lead the army's Southern Command shortly after his return from special duty in December 1969. His experience was needed in the escalating series of conflicts called the War of Attrition.

His first orders were to reinforce the Bar-Lev Line, the defensive plan he had so vehemently opposed. Putting aside his personal opinions, he began a massive road-building project that would allow tanks easy access to halt an invasion. Sharon was seen everywhere, supervising and encouraging his soldiers. With every Egyptian raid, Sharon responded with increasing force. Major Egyptian cities along the canal lay in ruins.

On May 30, 1970, Egyptian commandos ambushed an Israeli patrol and killed 18 soldiers. In response, Israeli aircraft shot down five Egyptian fighter planes flown by Soviet pilots. Nearly 270 Israelis died between March 1969 and August 1970, when a new cease-fire went into effect. Terrorism still continued in the Gaza Strip, and Sharon was sent to "establish order" there.

Sharon, in his usual careful manner, set out to solve the problem. He studied the area, taking note of specific places where terrorists could hide. He divided Gaza into manageable blocks with specific troops assigned to each one. He ordered trees cut down so that the Arab infiltrators couldn't hide behind them. He sent Arabic-speaking Israeli soldiers to mix with the Gaza residents and gain information about the terrorists and their hiding places. He ordered house-to-house searches and random stops of all Palestinian males. Gaza contained large refugee camps dating back to 1948 where there was strong support for anti-Israel activity. Sharon ordered curfews on refugee camp residents. This not only angered Palestinians but even some Israelis who criticized his harsh treatment of noncombatant men, women, and children.

Sharon's rough methods were often inconsiderate of the civilians in the area, but within seven months, his tactics dramatically cut down the number of terrorist attacks from the Gaza Strip. Sharon forcibly removed peaceful Arab groups from areas in northern Sinai as a security measure. At this time, Israel began a policy of allowing Jewish settlements in some areas of the West Bank and the Sinai. Some thought that Sharon expelled Arabs to make room for Jewish settlers.

The toughness of his tactics increased the hostility of Palestinians toward Israelis. Moshe Dayan, Israel's defense minister, appreciated the decrease in terror attacks but grew weary of defending Sharon's harsh tactics. Not wishing to remove Sharon from his position, Dayan diplomatically removed control of Gaza from the Southern Command and turned it over to the Central Command.

In January 1972, the new commander of the Israel Defense Forces, David Elazar, strongly suggested to Sharon that he should finally retire. Sharon's three-year term of command would not be renewed, he said, and there was no further chance of advancement. So in May 1973, Sharon officially resigned from the army. He requested that he be put in command of a reserve armored division. With financial help from American Jewish supporters, the Sharons bought Sycamore Farm, a run-down ranch in the northern Negev Desert. Here he could indulge in two favorite pastimes, farming and politics.

At a farewell party, he told his friends, "I have always maintained that a man must voice his opinions and then be willing to fight for them." Sharon was positioning himself as a candidate in the upcoming elections for seats in the Knesset. He displayed a less aggressive personality to the public. "Well, that's it," he told reporters on his arrival at the ranch. "Now I have to tend to the lambs, the sheep and the horses on my ranch. For 28 years I have been a soldier, but in the final analysis I am a farmer." But his pastoral life abruptly ended before it could really start.

The relative calm of the cease-fire period between Israel and Egypt, begun in 1970, was shattered at 2:00 P.M., October 6, 1973, on Yom Kippur, the holiest day of the Jewish year. Although Israel was aware of an Arab

military buildup, a simultaneous attack by Egypt and
Syria caught Israel by surprise. The start of the war
went badly for Israel. Casualties were high, and strate-
gies were lacking. Sharon received a call to report to
duty with his reserve armored unit. Hitching a ride in a
civilian truck, he arrived to find everything in disarray.
The highly vaunted Bar-Lev Line, opposed by Sharon
from the beginning, crumbled, and the Egyptian army
was advancing at an alarming rate into the Sinai.

The confusion and inaction of the general staff and
the conflicting orders from headquarters angered
Sharon. Frustrated at the lack of leadership, he ordered
his troops to regain a captured fortification site in spite
of an order from headquarters to stop. Sharon's unit
lost many tanks in the battle, and a call went out
demanding that he be relieved of his command.

While probing for an enemy soft spot, Sharon had
discovered an unprotected area at the Suez Canal
between two Egyptian armies. It was a place Israeli
troops and tanks could cross undetected. Sharon
pressed his superiors to allow him to cross and throw
the Egyptians off balance. Headquarters told him to
wait. On October 14, a massive Egyptian offensive
with 2,000 tanks took place in the Sinai against Israel.
In the largest tank battle since World War II, the Egyptians lost 250 tanks, but the Israelis lost only 6. It was
a major psychological and military victory for Israel.
Only then did Sharon receive permission to cross the
Suez Canal.

Israeli troops and tanks crossed the Suez Canal on a portable pontoon (float) bridge. Inset: *Major General Sharon,* right, *and another general confer over a map of the Sinai region in October 1973.*

Paratroopers crossed the canal in rubber dinghies, or small boats, under cover of darkness. Once a beachhead was established, Sharon crossed over with tanks and bulldozers, ferried on large, specially built rafts. Sharon's early optimistic reports to his superiors did not convey what was actually happening. Although initially unopposed by the Egyptians, Israeli casualties mounted, and fifty tanks were damaged as the Egyptians regrouped. At staff meetings, Sharon was widely criticized for not being forthcoming to his colleagues about his actions.

Still, within days, Israeli troops were able to lay a specially constructed portable bridge over the canal so that supplies and vehicles could cross. The timely arrival of military equipment and supplies from the

United States was a key to success. Israel made signifi-
cant advances on the Egyptian and Syrian fronts. The
Israelis had encircled Egypt's Third Army in the Sinai,
while other troops advanced to within fifty miles of
Cairo. Under pressure from the United States and the
Soviet Union, the UN adopted a resolution on October
22, requiring both sides to accept a cease-fire.

Sharon criticized his government for accepting the
resolution. He complained vehemently that more time
was needed to consolidate gains and completely force
all Egyptian soldiers back across the canal. Within the
few hours before the cease-fire was to go into effect,
Sharon urged the army to seize as much Egyptian ter-

*The Geneva, Switzerland, conference, held in December 1973 to
negotiate an end to the Yom Kippur War. The empty seats, lower
right, were for the Syrian delegation, who boycotted the talks.*

ritory as possible. He did not hold back his criticism of the conduct of the war. When he was reprimanded for not following orders, he yelled back, "Don't bother me with those things!" Clearly, his long-standing relationship with the army was coming to an end.

In January 1974, Lieutenant General Ariel Sharon took leave of his soldiers. He did not go quietly. In his final orders of the day to his soldiers, Sharon openly expressed his feelings about the war just ended and his plans for the future.

> The crossing of the canal brought us the victory in the war. If despite the blunders and the mistakes, despite the failures and obstructions, despite the loss of control and authority, we nevertheless achieved our victory, we must therefore recognize that this was the greatest victory the IDF has ever known. I promised to stay with you, but today I am forced to leave . . . and now I feel it is essential to fight on another front.

The Yom Kippur War changed the balance of power in the Middle East. It was clear that Israel could not easily be defeated. Nonetheless, Israel paid a heavy price in lives lost. The nation was in political turmoil after the war, and charges were made that the country had not been properly prepared. In the midst of the political upheaval, Ariel Sharon prepared to enter the battlefield of politics.

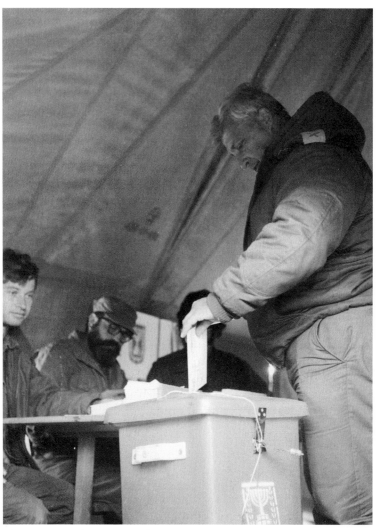

Sharon casts his vote in the December 1973 Israeli general elections. He was elected to the Knesset as a member of the Likud Party.

Chapter **FIVE**

FROM FIGHTER TO POLITICIAN

WITH THE WAR OVER, ARIEL SHARON FOCUSED ON the upcoming December 1973 elections. At a major political rally in Tel Aviv, crowds chanted "Arik, King of Israel." The chant was patterned on a popular Jewish song, "David, King of Israel," honoring Israel's biblical hero. Sharon won the election and took his place in the Knesset as a member of the Likud Party. Although the Labor Party, which had led Israel since 1948 won the overall election, the Likud managed to increase its representation in the Knesset.

During the upheavals after the nearly disastrous war, Prime Minister Golda Meir resigned and was replaced by Yitzhak Rabin. Sharon settled in as a member of parliament, but he had little patience for the endless

UNDERSTANDING ISRAELI ELECTIONS

srael's political system is based on European parliamentary democracy. There are three branches of government: the legislative, executive, and the judicial. Citizens over the age of eighteen can vote for members of the Knesset and the prime minister. The Knesset has 120 elected members. Election is by proportional representation. In this system, each of the many political parties presents a list of candidates to the public. On election day, voters select their favorite party. The number of candidates who are elected from each party depends on the proportion of votes cast for that party. A party must have at least 1.5 percent of the total vote to receive a Knesset seat. The seats are awarded to each party's candidates in order of their position on the list. Because of the low number of votes needed to win a seat, each election sees a large number of competing political parties. The two major parties are Labor and Likud.

The prime minister of Israel is elected separately. After the election, the president of Israel turns to the prime minister to form a government. Since Israel's birth in 1948, a single party has never won an outright majority of votes to rule the country. Intense backroom negotiations begin, and political deals are made with other parties until the prime minister is assured of a majority of at least sixty-one votes. This political system makes it possible for small single-agenda parties to wield more power than they probably deserve. Although elections are scheduled every four years, a new election can be held any time a vote of no confidence occurs.

debates and backroom politics. He spent much time alone or in the small office he shared with one of the Knesset's Arab members. Sharon enjoyed warm discussions with him on desert life and farming.

Sharon yearned to return to the army and action. The opportunity to do so presented itself in December 1974, when he was offered back his command. Sharon resigned from the parliament and resumed his military career in the Southern Command.

Back in the army, Sharon quickly found himself enmeshed in quarrels with his superiors. Again he loudly criticized and mocked their decisions. Rabin, the prime minister and a member of the Labor Party, appointed Sharon, a Likud member, as a special adviser on national security. For Rabin, this was a political move to control the outspoken Sharon while delicate peace negotiations continued with Egypt. Sharon saw this appointment as a possible way to reach the position of army chief of staff. Eight months later, though, Sharon resigned. He had played only a minor role within the government, and he realized that he would not be promoted.

Sharon returned to his farm. Although still a commander in the army reserves, he felt comfortable in the company of his Jewish and Arab workers. But this peaceful life, concerned only with farm animals and crop yields, quickly grew tiresome. With the help of some influential supporters, he founded the Shlomzion (Peace for Israel) Party. Sharon aligned himself with Gush Emunim, a deeply religious and highly nationalistic group that called for Jewish settlement in all of the biblical land of Israel, including the West Bank.

The 1977 election made history. For the first time since the establishment of Israel, a party other than the Labor Party—the Likud—would rule the country. The new prime minister was Menachem Begin.

During the election, Sharon was a highly visible candidate, but in true style, he alienated many voters with his gruff manner and undiplomatic comments. In the end, his new party won only two seats in the Knesset, including his. Begin invited Sharon to affiliate the tiny Shlomzion Party with the Likud, and Sharon accepted. In turn, Begin appointed Sharon to his cabinet as minister of agriculture.

In 1977 Anwar Sadat, the president of Egypt, made a historic visit to Israel in the quest for peace. Surprisingly, Menachem Begin, the hard-line leader, welcomed Sadat. Israelis were overjoyed. For the first time since 1948, the leader of an Arab country came to the Jewish state with an offer of peace. Sadat, who led Egypt during the 1973 war, greeted Israeli dignitaries at the airport. When he recognized Sharon, he said, "I tried to catch you at the Canal." Sharon, with a smile on his face, responded, "Now you have a chance to catch me as a friend."

"Had it not been for the crossing of the Canal," journalist Uri Dan wrote later, "Sadat would not have come to Israel on his peace mission." Although Sadat

Israeli prime minister Menachem Begin, right, *greets Egyptian president Anwar Sadat at Israel's Ben Gurion Airport in 1977. It was the first time in thirty years that an Israeli leader and an Arab leader had met to discuss the prospect of peace.*

and Begin were not even close to any meaningful agreements, they had broken the stalemate of years of hate.

The Egyptians wanted the return of all occupied lands lost in the 1967 war. Begin and the Likud leadership, including Sharon, were opposed to any "land for peace" deal. Even as negotiations began, Palestinian terrorists based in neighboring Arab countries continued to mount guerrilla attacks on Israel.

When he became agriculture minister in 1977, Sharon also became head of the Committee on Settlements.

He boldly announced the Sharon Plan to establish Jewish settlements throughout the West Bank. Prime Minister Begin, like Sharon, supported building towns and settlements there—facts on the ground—to make it difficult for Israel to return the land in exchange for peace.

Sharon saw that a major problem for the defense of Israel was that two-thirds of Jewish residents lived in a narrow strip of land along the Mediterranean coast. This population center could easily be attacked from high ground on the West Bank. Sharon wanted to ensure Israel's security by keeping control of these areas. To ensure that Jewish settlements on the West Bank prospered, he supervised the building of roads to connect them with other Israeli cities.

The vulnerability of Jerusalem, which was largely surrounded by West Bank land, also concerned him. Sharon began a process to encircle the city with a ring of Jewish towns and settlements. In the event of another war, these settlements would provide a security wall to protect the holy city. The image of bulldozers clearing land for new settlements spread around the world. Indeed, Sharon became known as "Bulldozer."

Within four years, Sharon succeeded in establishing more than sixty settlements, some no more than a few trailers and tents, in the West Bank. Many Israelis preferred to refer to this area by its biblical names, Judea and Samaria. Other settlements were created in Gaza and the Negev Desert to the south and the Golan Heights to the north. The establishment of settlements also had a political overtone, since much of Sharon's and Begin's support came from such groups as Gush Emunim.

By March 1978, negotiations with the Egyptians faltered, partly because of the settlement issue. Prime Minister Begin tried to defuse the problem by shifting responsibility for creating new settlements from Sharon's Committee on Settlements to the Committee on Defense. This did not deter Sharon, who continued to expand the number of settlements by simply calling them extensions to existing sites.

Yasser Arafat's Palestine Liberation Organization had been driven out of Jordan in 1970 because its violent protests against Israel threatened to destabilize the country. It set up new headquarters in Lebanon. Terrorist training camps operated freely there. Attacks on Israel increased along the long border shared with Lebanon. A six-mile security zone was established on the Lebanese border that extended north to the Litani River. UN troops were stationed there to keep the peace after the 1967 war. They were supposed to prevent PLO fighters from using the area to attack Israel, but the attacks continued because the PLO obtained sophisticated weapons that fired long distances. Northern Israeli towns were under constant attack from PLO missiles.

In early September 1978, hoping to keep alive the faltering agreement between Israel and Egypt, U.S. president Jimmy Carter invited Menachem Begin and Anwar Sadat to the presidential retreat, Camp David, in Maryland, to hammer out a peace treaty. Sharon was not invited. His blunt speaking and argumentative nature might hurt the delicate discussions. After twelve days, the Israelis agreed in principle to return the Sinai Peninsula to the Egyptians as part of a peace treaty. The only stumbling blocks were the Jewish settlements in the northern Sinai. Begin called Sharon to discuss this final issue. Surprisingly, Sharon advised Begin to give up the settlements in return for peace.

After months of ironing out details, Begin and Sadat signed the peace treaty on March 26, 1979, on the

Anwar Sadat, left, *and Menachem Begin,* right, *shake hands as U.S. president Jimmy Carter looks on. Meetings between the Arabs and Israelis took place in 1978 at Camp David, the U.S. presidential retreat in Maryland. The talks led to a peace treaty in March 1979.*

White House lawn in the presence of President Carter. In an emotional vote in the Knesset, Sharon voted with the majority to evacuate the settlements in the Sinai. In the 1981 Israeli elections, Menachem Begin's Likud Party was reelected. Ariel Sharon's popularity grew during the campaign, and when the prime minister formed his new government, Sharon was appointed minister of defense.

For all Israelis, the evacuation of the settlements in the Sinai was a traumatic time. They watched as thousands of Israeli soldiers moved out die-hard Israeli settlers who put up a last stand in the Sinai seaside town of Yamit in April 1982.

Without a single fatality on either side, Yamit was bulldozed and the Sinai was turned over to the Egyptians. Israel's southern borders were secured by a binding peace treaty. It was time for the country to turn its attention to the continuing problems in the north.

Yasser Arafat's Palestine Liberation Organization took control of Palestinian refugee camps in Lebanon beginning in 1968. Arafat, front, center, and supporters were photographed in Beirut, the capital of Lebanon, in 1982.

Chapter **SIX**

LEBANON, 1982

BY **1982 LEBANON WAS EMBROILED IN CIVIL WAR.** The once peaceful nation was fragmented into warring groups of Christians and Muslims. The Christian minority, which had coexisted with Muslims and flourished economically for generations, was under attack. The PLO—which began by taking over the Palestinian refugee camps in 1968—by the late 1970s had basically established a state within a state in Lebanon. In 1976 Syria was invited by the Christians to restore order. It quickly accepted, hoping to fulfill its own desire to absorb Lebanon into a larger Syria.

Strife-torn Lebanon became a center of revolutionary activity. Radical Palestinian paramilitary (not part of an official military) groups set up bases in the country from which to attack Israel. Soon the elected government of Lebanon was overwhelmed and fell apart. For Ariel Sharon, Lebanon was a top priority. He told a newspaper reporter, "Lebanon, in large part, has effectively been annexed by Syria; the world remains silent in the face of the massacre of the Lebanese Christians by the Muslims; and a large part of the country is ruled by terrorists."

Shortly after being named minister of defense, Sharon sought a plan to end the terrorist violence against Israelis from Lebanon. As part of the plan, he envisioned neutralizing the political and military power of the PLO in Beirut, Lebanon's capital; encouraging the Syrians to leave Lebanon; and restoring a workable Lebanese government. To that end, Israel allied itself with the Phalange—an important Christian militia group—and their leader Bashir Gemayel.

Sharon assured the United States that the plan would eradicate the danger to Israel from the terrorists in Lebanon without widening the conflict. On May 20, 1982, Alexander Haig, the U.S. secretary of state, said that the United States would support an invasion of Lebanon to clear terrorists from a twenty-five-mile area north of Israel. Sharon and Prime Minister Begin never revealed their true intent—to wipe out the PLO and force the Syrians out of the country. Israel also supported a parliamentary election to install Bashir Gemayel as president of Lebanon—with the assurance that Gemayel would formally establish peace with Israel.

When Palestinian terrorists in London severely wounded the Israeli ambassador to Great Britain on June 3, 1982, Israel responded with air attacks on PLO positions and offices in Lebanon. In turn, the PLO increased shelling of northern Israel. On June 6, an Israeli armored force crossed the Lebanese border to begin a large-scale military operation called Peace for Galilee. The area near the Sea of Galilee in northeastern Israel was a constant target of guerrilla attacks from across the Lebanese border.

The invasion had been approved a day earlier at an emergency cabinet meeting in Prime Minister Begin's home. The military action was to last no more than

Israeli defense minister Sharon, right, *rides with Israeli armored forces as they advance on the outskirts of Beirut, Lebanon, in June 1982.*

forty-eight hours and not exceed the twenty-five-mile corridor. Sharon, in fact, assured the cabinet members that the military plan would not involve Beirut or a direct attack on Syrian troops.

Sharon's promise of a routine but massive military operation soon fell apart. The rough mountainous terrain slowed troops, tanks, and supplies. Since the PLO had mixed with the local population, separating fighters from civilians was difficult. In addition, the threat to the Israeli air force from well-entrenched Syrian antiaircraft positions couldn't be ignored. On June 9, Sharon received permission to destroy Syrian missile bases. Israel's overwhelming superiority in the air virtually eliminated the Syrian air force in Lebanon. Dozens of Syrian fighters were shot down with few Israeli losses.

Sharon repeatedly asked the cabinet for permission to expand the war, each time citing a new need for escalation. It did not take long for Israelis to realize that the original scope of the war had been tremendously expanded. The twenty-five-mile barrier was forgotten as Israeli troops reached Beirut.

Other cabinet members accused Sharon of taking unapproved actions. The war had escalated, and the number of casualties had increased on both sides. Although the Israelis routinely tried to avoid striking noncombatants, civilian casualties mounted as bombs rained down on the Lebanese capital. Beirut, already heavily damaged by the civil war, experienced even further destruction.

Following heavy bombing of Beirut, Lebanon, Israeli soldiers enter a PLO hideout in Southern Beirut in 1982. Sharon's goal: force Arafat and the PLO from the city and other areas of Lebanon.

Israel pounded the Lebanese capital to dislodge the heavily entrenched PLO guerrillas hidden among innocent civilians. Day after day, television broadcasts showed the bloody images of war, including shots of women and children forced from their burning homes.

Sharon had maneuvered Prime Minister Begin and the cabinet into a position from which they could not retreat. At the gates of Beirut, Israeli forces began a two-month siege of the city to force Yasser Arafat and the PLO leadership out of the country. Even as negotiations began to evacuate Arafat and PLO fighters from Beirut, the fighting intensified. Shortages of food and electricity and the threat of constant air attacks affected everyone in the city. Newscasters worldwide reported on the harsh conditions, and many around the world criticized the Israeli actions. In spite of growing opposition to the war within Israel and criticism from his own government, Sharon intensified the pressure on Beirut.

After weeks of negotiations, a multinational force entered Beirut to supervise the removal of the PLO leaders. Yasser Arafat and his officials went to Tunisia in North Africa, and large numbers of fighters were absorbed into other Arab countries. PLO remnants blended into the civilian population. Sharon, at least in the short term, had eliminated the PLO leadership from Lebanon by interpreting orders to fit his needs. Many in Israel charged him with exceeding his authority. While Israel succeeded, at great human cost to both sides, in dislodging the PLO, Israel failed to convince the world of the importance of this mission and suffered a public relations disaster worldwide.

On August 23, the Lebanese parliament elected Bashir Gemayel, the Christian Phalangist leader and an Israeli ally, as president. Less than a month later, he was killed by an assassin's bomb. Tensions mounted, and Sharon received orders from Prime Minister Begin to enter Beirut and root out remaining PLO fighters, many of whom had fled to Palestinian refugee camps. Sharon worried that his soldiers would suffer a high casualty rate, so he requested that the

Christian Phalangist forces enter the Sabra and Shatilla refugee camps to look for hidden fighters. The Phalangists, angry at the death of their leader, were warned not to harm innocent civilians.

Phalangist militia entered the camps on the evening of September 16. As Israeli troops outside the camps fired mortars to illuminate the area, heavy shooting could be heard from inside. When the Phalangists finally exited the camps two days later, the Israelis realized that the Lebanese group had massacred hundreds of Palestinian civilians—men, women, and children. Television cameras broadcast the bloody aftermath worldwide. Although Lebanese Christians carried out the killings, Israel was blamed. Israel was in overall control of the camps and should have carefully monitored the actions of its Lebanese allies.

News of the massacre shocked the world and resulted in many anti-Israel demonstrations worldwide. In Tel Aviv, Israel, four hundred thousand people—nearly 10 percent of the population—took part in a demonstration against the massacre. Many blamed Sharon for leading the country into a disastrous war.

Cries for an investigation led to the appointment of a high-level commission headed by Yitzhak Kahan, the respected president of the Israeli Supreme Court. The commission took testimony from a number of witnesses. The Kahan Commission's report, released in February 1983, found that the Phalangist militia actually committed the massacre. But it said the Israeli army bore

Israeli protesters demonstrate against the involvement of Defense Minister Sharon and the Israeli army in the Sabra-Shatilla massacre in 1982, calling for a full investigation.

indirect responsibility by not foreseeing what would happen when enraged Christians were given open access to Muslim neighborhoods. "In our view," the report stated,"the Defense Minister made a grave mistake when he ignored the danger of acts of revenge and bloodshed by the Phalangists against the population in the refugee camps."

Ariel Sharon resigned as defense minister on February 14, 1983. He continued to deny the Kahan Commission's findings, saying "Israel bears no responsibility, either direct or indirect, for what happened there. This is an untruth which will be used by our enemies." He was quickly reappointed to the cabinet but had no specific duties. He spent much of his free time at his ranch with his family.

An ill Menachem Begin soon resigned as prime minister. He was replaced by Yitzhak Shamir. In the next election, on July 23, 1984, the Likud and Labor parties nearly split the votes and formed a National Unity Government. A decision was made that Shimon Peres of the Labor Party would serve as prime minister from 1984 to 1986, and Shamir of the Likud Party would serve from 1986 to 1988. Sharon received a call from Shamir inviting him to serve as minister of industry and trade.

One of Prime Minister Peres's first decisions was to withdraw Israeli forces from most of Lebanon and to confine remaining troops to a three- to six-mile security zone at the Israeli border to prevent terrorist incursions. Even though UN troops attempted to keep terrorists from infiltrating northern Israel, there were constant skirmishes there between Israeli soldiers and Palestinian guerrillas.

The cycle of Middle East violence extended to other sites. PLO terrorists killed Israeli visitors in Cyprus, shot up airports in Rome and Vienna, commandeered airliners, and hijacked a cruise ship in the Mediterranean, killing an elderly wheelchair-bound American. The PLO seemed to be controlled by violent extremists.

Ariel Sharon announces his resignation as minister of industry and trade and his interest in running for the office of prime minister of Israel in 1990.

Chapter **SEVEN**

NOT PEACE, NOT WAR

THROUGHOUT HIS LIFE, ARIEL SHARON WAS AN ambitious man always seeking career advancement. He believed that his country had to carry on its daily life in the "midst of a hundred million hostile people." He allied himself with nationalist groups that took a hard-line view of relations with Arab nations. Yet Sharon was also a practical person, who often adjusted his beliefs to fit political needs. He felt that for Israel "to survive we must be able to devise non-conventional solutions." From 1984 through 1996, he held nonmilitary cabinet positions that influenced key events in Israel.

In spite of ongoing violence with Palestinians, major changes were taking place in Israeli society. For six years after the Lebanon war, a national unity government ruled Israel. Although the Likud and Labor parties agreed on the need to remove troops from Lebanon, they could not reach common agreement on peace with the Palestinians.

Sharon's role in the government cabinets then reflected other challenges facing the country. In the early 1980s, the long-isolated Jewish population of Ethiopia began a difficult exodus to Israel. Famine, poor economic conditions, and religious persecution led them to immigrate. Most of the refugees arrived by massive airlifts kept secret by all parties so as not to inflame neighboring Arab countries. In ten years, the Jewish Ethiopian population of Israel reached twenty-eight thousand.

The later years of Ethiopian arrivals coincided with the beginnings of a larger mass immigration of Jews from the Soviet Union. One year almost two hundred thousand refugees from the Soviet Union arrived in Israel. They faced a severe housing shortage. New arrivals had to be temporarily housed in hastily assembled tent and trailer sites. In his usual blunt style, Sharon saw the problem and set out to solve it. Ignoring financial problems that could affect the country's economy, he built apartments throughout Israel and especially in the West Bank.

As early as 1977, Sharon had announced an ambitious goal of settling two million Jews in the West Bank. "If we want a strong independent state we must give up settling just on the coastal strip and move elsewhere. Otherwise, Israel would consist of a mass of concrete . . . all within the range of Arab guns." The arrival of masses of Jews from the Soviet Union provided an opportunity to put his idea into action.

In December 1987, young Palestinians, disillusioned with their leadership and the growth of Israeli settlements, began a popular uprising—the intifada—against Israeli occupation in the West Bank and Gaza. They reflected a larger Palestinian feeling of despair as they watched the number of Jewish settlements grow on land the UN resolution had set aside for them. Armed mainly with stones, young people attacked Israeli soldiers, who responded to the spontaneous rebellion with bullets, curfews, and arrests. As the intifada escalated and became a way of life, the number of Palestinian casualties rose. Israel found itself fighting a battle on two fronts: the streets of the West Bank and Gaza and the world's news media, which showed the world photos of armed Israeli troops battling stone-throwing Palestinians. To make the point that Jews could live anywhere, Ariel Sharon bought an apartment in the area of Jerusalem where most Muslim's lived, further flaming tensions.

Sensing the intifada as a remarkable opportunity to shape events, the PLO took control of the disorganized stone throwers and turned the intifada into a full-scale political campaign to achieve a Palestinian state in the West Bank and Gaza. More than twenty thousand people on both sides were killed or injured between 1987 and 1993. The intensity of the violence convinced a growing number of Israelis that the time had arrived to engage the Palestinians in peace negotiations.

Although some factions of the Palestine Liberation Organization, such as the group called Hamas, supported increased terrorism against Israel, most groups within the PLO also agreed with their leader, Yasser Arafat, of the need to pursue peace. It would not be easy. Few Israelis fully trusted the Palestinians, and few Palestinians trusted Israelis. At a PLO meeting in Algeria on November 15, 1988, the organization voted to recognize Israel, renounce terrorism, and accept a UN resolution that called for an exchange of territory for peace. Shortly thereafter, however, Palestinian terrorists launched an unsuccessful raid on Israel. Israeli voters, wary of Palestinian actions, reelected Yitzhak Shamir and his hard-line Likud Party.

Ariel Sharon, the minister of trade and industry, watched the increasing violence and grew frustrated at the ineffectiveness of Israel's military response to the intifada. He told *Time* magazine "If cars and buses were attacked daily by...bombs or stones for 16 months in Washington, could you imagine it would be tolerated?...What would happen in the U.S. to terrorists who are not citizens? In less than 24 hours, they would be rounded up, taken to the airport and expelled. I would round up the terrorists here and expel them. Immediately!"

PLO leader Yasser Arafat declared Palestine an independent state at a meeting of the Palestine National Council in November 1988. He also announced that the PLO would recognize the nation of Israel and renounce terrorism.

During the same interview, the reporter asked if he would someday like to be prime minster. Sharon answered, "I have the desire. I know I could do the job. I know I would do it as it should be done. At the same time, I have much less ambition than people think. That is my secret weapon. I could be out of the government tomorrow without a minute of crisis. My strength does not come from political life. It comes from my family, the land, and my farm. I have a lot of things I want very much to do and would never be bored doing them."

But Prime Minister Shamir was not about to resign. He was engaged in a difficult debate with the United States on ways to bring peace to the Middle East. Shamir's plan called for Palestinian elections and negotiations with the PLO over the occupied West Bank and Gaza. Although Shamir was deeply protective of Israel, he was not tough enough for Sharon, who called for the government to "eliminate the heads of the terrorist organizations, first of all Arafat."

On February 19, 1990, Ariel Sharon resigned as a member of Yitzhak Shamir's cabinet and announced, "I certainly see myself as a candidate for Prime Minister." He publicly derided Shamir's peace plan, saying "The plan by itself is a mistake. It will not bring us peace, but will lead to more tension and more bloodshed and maybe even to a war which all of us would like to prevent." At a mass Likud meeting, Sharon turned to Shamir and said, "Under your government, Palestinian terrorism runs wild throughout the land of Israel. . . . I know it is possible to eliminate terror," he insisted.

Alliances shift quickly in Israeli politics. With the reelection of Shamir, Sharon was named minister of construction and housing. While his views on dealing with the intifada had not changed, he tackled his new position with fervor. He initiated programs to absorb immigrants in a building boom such as never had been seen before in Israel. Within a few years, more than 140,000 new apartments were built and more than 20,000 renovated.

The administration of George H. W. Bush snubbed Sharon on his diplomatic visit to Washington in May 1991. The U.S. secretary of housing refused to allow him in his office, choosing instead to meet him at the Israeli Embassy. The United States was upset not only by Sharon's views against any negotiations with the Palestinians but also by his continuing expansion of Jewish settlements on the West Bank.

Sharon ordered thousands of prefabricated houses and developed new communities, particularly in the West Bank. The Israeli Supreme Court soon ruled that Sharon's actions exceeded his authority, since they were largely carried out without cabinet approval. Nonetheless, the model had been created, and few politicians were willing to retract Sharon's initiative.

The arrival of so many people within a short period also affected poor Israelis who found their rent costs rising. Tent camps began appearing around the country. When he presented a temporary-housing plan to the cabinet, Sharon said, "We must provide an immediate answer for the homeless and for the immigrants. There is no room for compromise."

Ironically, another war in the region led to the start of meaningful negotiations. On August 2, 1990, Iraq invaded its neighbor Kuwait. A coalition of nations, led by the United States, sent troops to the region and began military action against Iraq on January 16, 1991. During Operation Desert Storm, the Iraqis launched missiles at Israel, a country not involved in the war. Israel, at the insistence of the United States, did not respond with military action. The United States knew that Arab members of the coalition would have pulled out of the war if their enemy, Israel, became involved.

At the successful conclusion of the war, Secretary of State James Baker convinced leaders of Middle Eastern countries to join the United States in a special conference in Madrid, Spain. Although the Madrid Conference marked the first time Israel was able to sit at a negotiations table with Arab nations, Sharon blamed the United States for "deliberately humiliating Israel and pressing it to make concessions that jeopardize its survival."

With another election upcoming in Israel, Sharon again voiced his displeasure with Prime Minister Shamir and the United States' proposal for a peace conference. "I am not speaking of running against someone but about a challenge for us to conduct proper policy," Sharon said. With the intifada still raging, Sharon argued for a heavier response by Israel to crush the Palestinian uprising. He promised "a proper policy for security, which can be restored to Israel." When two hundred armed Jewish settlers raided an Arab neighborhood in East Jerusalem, Sharon supported them saying, "We are talking here about the rights of Jews to live in Jewish homes . . . in the capital of Israel."

Yitzhak Shamir lost the July 1992 election, and Yitzhak Rabin of the Labor Party became the new prime minister. Rabin quickly told the United States that Israel "will do its utmost to promote the peace-keeping efforts... under the Madrid framework." On August 20, 1993, after fourteen secret meetings between Israelis and Palestinians in Oslo, Norway, both sides signed a Declaration of Principles to seek peace.

Arafat sent a letter to Israel's foreign minister, Shimon Peres, renouncing terrorism and confirming the "right of the State of Israel to exist in peace and security." On September 13, 1993, under the auspices of the new U.S. president, Bill Clinton, Yasser Arafat and Yitzhak Rabin signed a peace treaty on the White House lawn in Washington. Israel withdrew from Gaza, and terrorism subsided dramatically, but not completely. Yasser Arafat returned to Gaza after years of exile to plan for a Palestinian state. Less than a year later, Israel signed a formal peace treaty with Jordan. For many, though violence had not completely subsided, it was a glorious time filled with hope.

The Likud, now the opposition party, began looking for a new leader. Sharon offered himself. In spite of his popularity among a large segment of the population, particularly West Bank settlers and Jewish immigrants from Arab countries, polls showed that he would lose. He withdrew from the election, and U.S.-educated Benjamin Netanyahu became head of the Likud Party.

Sharon remained in the Knesset but without a leadership role. Although no longer a cabinet member, he

did not shy away from public statements about a foreign policy that he opposed. As Israeli troops turned
control of six major West Bank cities to the Palestinians as part of the peace agreement, Sharon continued
to champion the expansion of existing settlements. "I
hope you will see," he told reporters, "that it is busi-
ness as usual here. Even now with limitations and
restrictions, construction is going on. There is much to
do in the coming years." He insisted, "This area cannot
and never will be under Palestinian rule." His own
peace plan called for no further land to be handed over
to the Palestinians and for Israel to maintain the right
to enter Palestinian territory to chase down terrorists.
Even as he publicly refused to legitimatize the Palestinian leadership, Sharon maintained secret contacts with
a few Palestinian representatives over the years. In
spite of his warnings that he would never shake hands
with Arafat, he once accepted the gift of an antique
dagger with a Hebrew inscription sent by the Palestinian leader.

At 9:40 P.M. on Saturday, November 4, 1995, a young
man assassinated Prime Minister Yitzhak Rabin.
Stunned Israelis were shocked to learn that the murderer was not a Palestinian but a right-wing Jewish law
student, who thought Rabin had gone too far to make
peace with the Palestinians. Rabin was succeeded by
his foreign minister, Shimon Peres. In spite of the
peace agreement signed by Rabin and Arafat, terrorists,
including a growing number of Palestinian suicide

bombers, had killed nearly two hundred Israelis. In the May 1996 elections, Likud leader Benjamin Netanyahu defeated Peres.

Most Israelis yearned for meaningful peace. But many felt that Rabin and Peres had moved too quickly in making concessions to the Palestinians, without receiving real guarantees for an end to violence. They elected Netanyahu who, although publicly committed to the agreements already in place with the Palestinians, was opposed to the creation of an independent Palestinian state. Netanyahu appointed Sharon to a newly created cabinet post, minister of national infrastructure. In this role, Sharon gained control of the economy, including energy, water, public land administration, road building, and rural construction.

This position enabled him to pursue the expansion of existing Jewish settlements. By 1996, 130,000 Jews lived amid 2 million Arabs in the West Bank and Gaza, and Sharon wanted to double the number. Even as new negotiations were to begin on an agreement on settlements, Sharon wanted to ensure an expansion of existing settlements, linking them by roads and highways. Sharon's plan would make it difficult, if not impossible, for a Palestinian state to be carved out of what was left of the West Bank.

Two years later, Prime Minister Netanyahu added the important position of foreign minister to Sharon's responsibilities. The appointment took place just prior to a U.S.-sponsored summit meeting between Israel and the Palestinians at the Wye Plantation in Maryland. The meeting was to focus on additional Israeli withdrawals. Some thought that Sharon's participation could mean an end to the peace process. Others thought that with his tough views, he would actually bring progress to the negotiating table.

Both sides wanted to make progress. The Palestinians wanted an independent state. The Israelis wanted a meaningful peace and an end to the terrorist violence. U.S. president Bill Clinton called both sides together to restart the badly damaged peace process and succeeded in hammering together a new interim agreement. Although nothing new was added from previous agreements, it kept the peace process and the concept of land for peace alive.

Yasser Arafat, left, *and Ariel Sharon,* right, *both attended a peace conference organized by U.S. president Bill Clinton at Wye Plantation in Maryland in October 1998.*

Sharon publicly supported Netanyahu and the peace plan. When a reporter asked him how he felt, he answered, "I was the father of settlements, if I may boast this title, and today, I also see myself as the father of settlement." He went on to explain that he felt the pain of the settlers who would have to move, but this was a necessary step to make "a sincere and genuine effort to . . . attain peace."

In November 1998, Sharon met with Palestinian official Mahmoud Abbas to conclude the first stage of an agreed-upon Israeli withdrawal from the West Bank and the release of Palestinian prisoners held by Israel. "We are starting today to negotiate the permanent agreement," Sharon told reporters. Sharon explained to Knesset members that the Wye River agreement was "the least of all evils and the best that could be achieved." In truth, both sides found that enforcing details of the agreement was almost impossible.

In the next national election, Israelis rejected the hard-line politics of Benjamin Netanyahu and the Likud and elected Ehud Barak of the Labor Party as prime minister. Sharon took on the leadership of the Likud, but few expected him to actually seek the prime minister's office in the next election.

As political infighting continued, Ariel Sharon suffered a great loss at home. His beloved wife Lily died of lung cancer on March 25, 2000, at the age of sixty-three. She had been at his side continually, encouraging and supporting him. Sharon was now seventy-two years old.

At an age when many people retired to focus on family and grandchildren, Sharon plunged himself deeper into political work.

On Thursday morning, September 28, 2000, a day before the beginning of Rosh Hashanah, the Jewish New Year, Ariel Sharon took a walk. Protected by one thousand armed soldiers and police officers, Sharon strolled for an hour on the Temple Mount in Jerusalem. "It is the right of any Jew to visit the Temple Mount, Judaism's holiest shrine," Sharon said. Others disagreed. Stone-throwing Palestinians yelling, "Murderer, get out!" clashed with Israeli police.

As he took his walk, Sharon proclaimed, "The Temple Mount is in our hands and will remain in our hands." He was remembering the time from 1948 to 1967 when Jews could not visit their holy places. Then the sites were under the control of Jordan. When Israel took control of the entire city in 1967, it opened access to the religious sites in Jerusalem. Christian, Jewish, and Muslim groups are allowed to visit and maintain their specific sites, but Israelis have the right to go anywhere in Jerusalem. Sharon said he was testing that right with his controversial walk.

Others saw the walk differently. Yasser Arafat declared Sharon's visit "provocative and dangerous." An Arab member of the Knesset saw the visit as an effort to "flare up the area and to burn up the place."

Violence between Arabs and Jews escalated after Sharon's walk. Since that September, Palestinian suicide

In September 2000, Ariel Sharon, left center, *visits the Temple Mount in Jerusalem, which is also the site of the al-Aqsa Mosque. Palestinians hurled rocks at Israeli troops in protest of Sharon's controversial visit to the site, holy to both Jews and Muslims.*

bombers have killed hundreds of Israelis and wounded thousands more. Israelis were terrified. Life for Palestinians also became unbearable as Israelis responded with targeted killings of terrorist leaders, the use of helicopter gunships, the invasions of Palestinian areas, and the destruction of Palestinian homes.

Meanwhile, President Bill Clinton, whose term in office was ending, tried again to bring the Israelis and Palestinians together at Camp David to reach a final and binding agreement. Barak attempted to end the conflict by making new concessions including the division of of Jerusalem, something no Israeli government had previously dared to consider. Despite this, Arafat refused to continue negotiations. A new and more violent intifada was under way.

Prime minister-elect Sharon following his landslide victory over Ehud Barak in February 2001.

Chapter **EIGHT**

THE PRIME MINISTER

ARIEL SHARON WAS ELECTED PRIME MINISTER OF THE State of Israel in February 2001. The seventy-two-year-old soldier won in a landslide. Israelis still mistrusted the Palestinians and thought former prime minister Barak's Camp David offer was too generous, especially the division of Jerusalem. They objected to giving away land without a firm and meaningful commitment to peace by the Palestinians. Terrorist acts, particularly against Israeli civilians, had grown in number and ferocity, especially suicide bombings.

Sharon's rough image and his tough reputation led many to doubt his playing a role as a peacemaker. Many countries held negative views about him. Newspapers returned to the events at Sabra and Shatilla or referred to him as "the butcher Sharon." Many people blamed the new uprising on Ariel Sharon's walk on the Temple Mount. Yet, in his victory speech, Sharon said, "I know peace requires difficult compromises— on both sides. I am calling on our Palestinian neighbors to leave violence behind and come back to a way of negotiations and solving arguments between us in methods of peace."

Ariel Sharon fought in each of Israel's many wars, rising in rank and importance. He was known as much for his independence and daring as for his frequent dislike of his superior officers. Yet he was always committed to the security of his country. To those who were quick to label him a "warmonger," he once said, "I believe I can make peace because I saw all the horrors of wars. I participated in all the wars and lost my best friends in battles. I was seriously injured twice. Therefore, I understand the importance of peace better than the politicians who speak about peace but never experienced war."

Because of his reputation, many expected Sharon to take an immediate and decisive military stand against the Palestinians. Instead, he used his first few months in office to await the results of negotiations led by the United States. Attacks on civilians continued. The United States called on both sides to accept a cease-fire and for Israel to stop building or expanding settlements in the West Bank. Sharon rejected the plea, saying that the settlements were "a vital national enterprise." Sharon said that he would only begin negotiating with the Palestinians after a seven-day period in which there were no attacks on Israeli civilians. No lull in the violence occurred.

In early June, a suicide bomber killed twenty-one young Israelis at a nightclub in Tel Aviv. Two months later, fifteen men, women, and children died in a suicide bombing of a popular Jerusalem pizza restaurant. After each attack, Arafat publicly condemned the violence. Israelis and others, thought he was either unwilling or unable to reign in the terrorists.

In August, after yet another suicide bombing, this time in Haifa, Ariel Sharon ordered temporary occupation of territory that had been turned over to the Palestinians in 1994. Sharon said that if Arafat could not or would not stop the terrorists, Israel had no choice but to move in.

On September 11, 2001, members of al-Qaeda, a terrorist group based in Afghanistan, attacked the World Trade Center Towers in New York and the Pentagon in Washington, D.C., killing nearly three thousand people. President George W. Bush sought to include Arab nations in a coalition of partners to fight the terrorists in Afghanistan. He needed Israel to maintain a low profile as it had a decade earlier during Operation Desert Storm in Kuwait. Sharon remained adamant. The deployment of Israeli troops in the West Bank would continue, he explained to a reporter. "We are in a war here, a special kind of war."

A few days after the September 11 attack, Arafat reaffirmed his commitment to yet another cease-fire and ordered his security forces not to fire on Israeli troops. Sharon ordered a gradual military withdrawal from Palestinian territory. Israeli and Palestinian negotiators agreed on a short period of time without attacks on Israeli civilians for negotiations to continue. The agreement was ended almost immediately with a Palestinian attack in which two Israelis died and fourteen were injured. On the same day, October 2, Bush declared for the first time—in large measure to placate Arab allies—that the United States was prepared to back the creation of an independent Palestinian state.

On October 17, terrorists entered a Jerusalem hotel and assassinated Rehavam Zeevi, an Israeli cabinet member and minister of tourism. In response, Sharon sent tanks and troops into major cities of the West Bank in the most far-reaching takeover yet.

Ariel Sharon was angry. He warned Arafat that terrorist groups of the PLO had escalated the unofficial war to a point of no return. Bush agreed and demanded that Arafat do more to stop the near-daily violence against Israelis. To make the point, Sharon ordered the bombing of Arafat's offices in Gaza City. After another deadly bombing of Israelis on December 12, Sharon finally concluded that Arafat was not interested in peace and broke off all ties with him. Israel attacked Palestinian buildings on the West Bank and surrounded Arafat's headquarters in Ramallah. Again,

When Israel attacked Gaza City in December 2001, Yasser Arafat's PLO offices, above, were a key target for Israeli missiles.

Arafat issued an order to end suicide bombings, but to Sharon and President Bush this was just one more hollow gesture.

On January 5, 2002, the Israeli navy captured a Palestinian-crewed ship, the *Karine A*, heading to Gaza with fifty tons of arms and ammunition. Arafat's previous proclamations of peaceful intentions were exposed as false when Israel put the ship's cargo on public display. The suicide bombings of civilians continued as Israel intensified its attacks on Palestinian cities. The casualties on both sides were then in the thousands, with no end in sight. A particularly frustrated Sharon told an Israeli newspaper that he regretted not having "eliminated" Arafat twenty years earlier, when he forced the Palestinian leader out of Beirut.

On March 29, 2002, Israeli tanks and bulldozers attacked Arafat's compound in Ramallah. In spite of all the bloodshed in this round of violence, Sharon said this marked the start of a "long and complicated war that knows no borders." Arafat was personally not targeted, but he was isolated in his compound by the Israelis and kept from public view. Once more, Bush called on him to end the bloodshed, blaming him directly for the suicide bombings. Sharon declared Arafat an "enemy of Israel."

Sharon believed he had no choice but to do what Arafat did not—send troops to uproot the "infrastructure of terrorism." By June 2002, Israel had reoccupied seven important cities in the West Bank. The occupation of Bethlehem and Jenin attracted worldwide attention. In Bethlehem nearly two hundred Palestinian gunmen invaded the Church of the Nativity, believed to be the birthplace of Jesus. Israeli troops lay siege to the building. In Jenin thirteen Israeli soldiers were killed in an ambush as they fought through narrow congested alleys to root out hidden Palestinian gunmen. Arafat inflamed world opinion against Israel by accusing the Israelis of massacring thousands of innocent men, women, and children in Jenin. Although the charges later proved to be false, Israel's international reputation was further damaged. Sharon was furious with the Palestinians. "They look you in the eye and lie," he said.

In a live television broadcast, Sharon stated, "The State of Israel, under my direction, made all the efforts to arrive at a cease-fire. Everything we received in return for our efforts was terrorism, terrorism and more terrorism. Our hand is and always will be extended for peace with the Palestinian people but no one should be deluded. Our extended hand does not mean that we will give in to terrorism or to terrorists." On September 18, the United States, the UN, the European Union, and Russia joined together as the Quartet to propose a road map to peace with the goal of establishing a Palestinian state living in peace alongside Israel. Yet militant Palestinian groups responded with even more suicide bombings.

Israelis felt helpless. Ehud Barak, had offered the Palestinians nearly everything they wanted. The result was a degree of terrorism never before seen. Sharon responded to the violence with strong force. As casualties mounted on both sides and the economic situation for Palestinians reached a new low, there seemed to be no future for peace. When Labor members of Sharon's cabinet quit in frustration, Sharon had to call for a new election in January 2003. He easily won.

Under intense pressure from Sharon and Bush, Yasser Arafat reluctantly agreed to appoint a prime minister. Since Israel and the United States refused to deal directly with Arafat, they hoped this official could pave the way for meaningful negotiations. Sharon welcomed the appointment of Mahmoud Abbas as prime minister and met with him for preliminary discussions. Within a month, the three-month cease-fire, called for by the road map to peace, was shattered by yet another suicide bombing in Haifa that took fifteen lives. Sharon, seeing no hope, began a policy of targeting terrorist leaders for assassination.

Sharon began a controversial fence-building project to separate the West Bank from Israel to keep terrorists out. He had once opposed the idea, but the alarming number of suicide bombings caused him to change his mind. Many Palestinians and Israelis thought the fence was a bad idea, since it might influence the future borders of a Palestinian state.

Seeing no immediate chance of engaging Palestinian leaders in meaningful negotiations, Ariel Sharon made

Prime Minister Sharon, left center, *shakes hands with opposition leader Shimon Peres, after the Knesset approved Sharon's plan to dismantle Jewish settlements in Gaza in February 2004.*

FENCES AND NEIGHBORS

I n 2002, frustrated with the continuation of suicide bombings and a lack of progress on the diplomatic front, Ariel Sharon approved a 425-mile barrier to divide Israel from the West Bank. The purpose was to prevent terrorists from entering Israel. The first phase was completed in July 2003. The intended route of the barrier put chunks of Palestinian land on the Israeli side of the barrier in order to include the Jewish settlements on the West Bank. As construction of the barrier—a linking of barbed-wire fences, concrete walls, and ditches—proceeded, international objections led to court decisions in Israel to reroute the wall closer to Israel's pre-1967 borders. A nonbinding opinion of the World Court in 2004 concluded that the wall violated international law.

Israelis largely supported the barrier as the number of suicide bombings decreased. Palestinians complained that the barrier separated them from their fields, schools, and families. They feared that construction of the barrier was a one-sided Israeli attempt to mark out the boundary of a future Palestinian state.

a surprising decision in 2004 to dismantle most Jewish settlements in Gaza and remove both settlers and soldiers. This act perplexed his supporters. Yet no one should have been too surprised. Ariel Sharon, after all, has been confounding friends and foes his entire life. In spite of formal objections from his Likud Party, Sharon vowed to continue the withdrawal plans.

Ariel Sharon in December 2004

Chapter **NINE**

THE FUTURE

ALTHOUGH HE WAS ALWAYS AN IMPOSING-LOOKING man, the older Ariel Sharon seems almost grandfatherly. He also seems to have mellowed over the years. He is more open to suggestions and other people's opinions. One thing that has not changed is his continuing commitment to the safety and well-being of the State of Israel. Speaking to American Jewish leaders, he said, "Jews have this one, tiny country. It is the only place in the world where Jews have the right and privilege to defend themselves. Israel will not be able to make any compromises when it comes to our security."

Looking back on his life, one sees a person with a reputation for tough-mindedness and individualism. He has tended to ignore orders from superiors and do what he believed to be the right thing. Surprisingly, many of his most criticized past actions also turned out to be correct.

The man who throughout his life has battled with Arabs and fully supported the building and expansion of Jewish settlements in the West Bank and Gaza made a revealing comment to the Knesset during the bloodiest days of the al-Aqsa Intifada in June 2003. His Likud supporters couldn't believe it when he told them "the occupation [of Palestinian territory] can't go on." It was "bad for us and them." His use of the word *occupation* marked a dramatic departure from the belief he had often supported that the West Bank would always belong to Israel.

While maintaining that there could be no peace as long as terror against civilians continues, Sharon remains optimistic. In a speech on August 13, 2003, before a group of Jewish young people visiting Israel, he reflected on Israel's past with hope for the future.

"When I look at what we have done here in the last 55 years, I am optimistic, and I think that all of us can be optimistic. Though we were holding the sword in one hand, not because we wanted to, but we did not have another way, during all those years, we had tremendous achievements here. We managed to develop one of the most sophisticated industries, we have centers of research and science known world-wide, we brought to Israel millions of Jews from 102 countries, speaking 82 languages, and all of them speak or learn Hebrew, the language of the Bible. With all the problems that we have, we live in a wonderful country."

Much of Sharon's life has been spent defending his country. On Israel's Memorial Day in 2003, he stood in a cemetery before the families of soldiers with whom he fought in the 1948 war. "Behind me," he said, "was a mass grave of our company, and also there a great part of my platoon." He had barely survived and never forgot the horror of battle.

Ariel Sharon continues to evoke controversy. While he has many admirers, others continue to revile him and

Ultra-Orthodox Israeli Jews pass in front of a poster criticizing Sharon's plan to move Jewish settlers from Gaza in 2004. A controversial leader, Sharon draws supporters and critics.

THE DEATH OF YASSER ARAFAT

Yasser Arafat, Ariel Sharon's longtime enemy, died on November 11, 2004, in a Paris hospital after a long illness. Since the beginning of the al-Aqsa Intifada and the terror attacks on Israel, which Sharon blamed directly on Arafat, the Palestinian leader had been isolated physically and diplomatically by Israel, with the support of the United States, in the West Bank city of Ramallah. Without mentioning Arafat's name, Sharon responded to news of the Palestinian leader's death by saying, "the recent events could be a historic turning point for the Middle East. Israel is a country that seeks peace and will continue its efforts to reach a peace deal with the Palestinians without delay."

To Sharon, Arafat was a dangerous terrorist "whose hands are stained with blood." Even when Israel and the Palestinians signed the Oslo Accords in 1993 as a first step toward eventual peace, Sharon refused to believe in Arafat's sincerity. To Sharon, Arafat was simply a "criminal."

Even before Arafat's death, Sharon began implementing unilateral plans to withdraw Jewish settlers from Gaza. With the emergence of new Palestinian leadership, hope rose for a return to negotiations using the road map to peace endorsed by the United States, Russia, the European Union, and the United Nations.

call him a butcher or mass murderer. To many, the real Sharon is the man who led the raid on Qibya in 1953 and invaded Lebanon in 1982. Some people had even brought war crimes charges against him for the Sabra and Shatilla massacres in Lebanon. He referred to those charges as politically inspired, and though they were eventually dismissed, they remain embarrassments.

For someone who is constantly in the public eye, Sharon's private life is his refuge. As a child, he lived in a home with few outward displays of affection. As he grew older, he found warmth and support in the camaraderie of military life. Remembering his own love-starved childhood, Sharon has been a supportive father to his sons and remains close to them.

His refuge is Sycamore Farm. There amid the eight hundred acres of orange groves and grazing herds of sheep and cattle, he relaxes and puts aside political and military problems. Pointing through a large picture window to the lush green fields, he told a recent visitor, "My strength has nothing to do with political apparatus. I get my strength from nature, from flowers. . . .

I feel all the ties and roots of the Jewish people in this place. There has been nonstop Jewish life here for thousands of years. That is what I stand for. This is not a campaign. It's a war for survival. The Jews have one, tiny, small country. We demand only one thing: to live peacefully. We have the right and the ability to defend ourselves and we will never give up. It is our duty. That is what I feel."

TIMELINE

1897 The first Zionist Congress, led by Theodor Herzl, lays the groundwork for reestablishing a Jewish state after two thousand years of exile.

1917 The Balfour Declaration by the British government formally supports the establishment of a Jewish state in Palestine.

1928 Ariel Scheinerman (Ariel Sharon) is born on February 27 in Kfar Malal.

1945 World War II and the Holocaust ends.

1948 The State of Israel is born. Israel's War of Independence begins.

1956 The Sinai War, the second Arab-Israeli War begins.

1964 The Palestine Liberation Organization (PLO) is founded.

1967 Israel defeats Egypt, Jordan ,and Syria in the Six-Day War.

1973 Egypt and Syria attack Israel, starting the Yom Kippur War.

1977 Anwar Sadat of Egypt visits Israel.

1979 Egypt and Israel sign a peace treaty.

1982 Israel invades Lebanon.

1987 The first intifada begins.

1988 Yasser Arafat and the PLO renounce terrorism.

1991 The Persian Gulf War is fought. The Madrid Peace Conference is held.

1993 Secret meetings in Oslo, Norway, lead to agreement by Israel and the PLO to recognize each other.

2000 The second intifada begins after Ariel Sharon visits the Temple Mount.

2001 Ariel Sharon is elected prime minister of Israel.

2004 Ariel Sharon announces a plan to withdraw nearly all Israeli settlements and soldiers from Gaza. The building of a security barrier to separate Israel from the Palestinian territories creates international furor.

SOURCES

8 Ariel Sharon, and David Chanoff, *Warrior: An Autobiography* (New York: Simon and Schuster, 1989), 57.

8 Ibid., 67.

12 Ibid., 15.

14 Ibid., 10.

15 Ibid., 27.

16 Ibid., 30.

18 Norman H. Finkelstein, *Friends Indeed: The Special Relationship of Israel and the United States* (Brookfield, CT: Millbrook Press, 1989), 40.

22 Matti Shavitt, *On the Wings of Eagles* (Tel Aviv: Olive Books, 1970), 26.

26 Ibid., 31.

26 Ibid., 39.

27 Uzi Benziman, *Sharon: An Israeli Caesar* (New York: Adama, 1985), 58.

27 Sharon, 119–120.

28 Ibid., 88.

31 Herbert Druks, *The US and Israel, 1945–1973* (New York: Speller, 1979), 61.

31 Benziman, 74.

38 Finkelstein, 74.

39 Sharon, 83.

40 Ibid., 201.

40 Shavitt, 53.

42 Sharon, 213–214.

44 Ibid., 223.

47 Benziman, 125.

47 Ibid., 126.

51 Ibid., 174–175.

56 Sharon, 376.

64 Benziman, 230.

70 William E. Smith, "The Verdict Is Guilty," *Time* (February 21, 1983): 26.

70 "Impact of Israel's Turmoil," *US News and World Report*,
    February 21, 1983, 22.

73 Sharon, 531.

75 Colin Schindler, *The Land beyond Promise* (London:
    Tauris, 1989), 285.

76 Murray J. Gart, "Never! Never! Never!" *Time* (April 17,
    1989): 40.

78 "Eliminate Arafat, Sharon Demands," *Boston Globe*, July
    18, 1989, 45.

78 "Hysteria on the Right," *Time* (February 26, 1990): 30.

78 "Sharon Formally Resigns," *Boston Globe*, February 19,
    1990, 2.

79 "Sharon Requesting NIS 2.7B for PreFabs, Rent
    Subsidies," *Jerusalem Post*, July 24, 1990, 1.

80 "Soft with Some, Tough on Others," *Jerusalem Post*,
    December 12, 1991, 6.

80 "Settlements Won't Stop, Says Sharon," *Jerusalem Post*,
    July 3, 1991, 1.

85 "Sharon Takes Aim at US in New Power Bid," *Boston
    Globe*, October 13, 1991, 2.

85 Ethan Bronner, "Sharon Upbeat despite West Bank
    Transfer," *Boston Globe*, November 17, 1995, 2.

85 Report, Channel 3, Israel TV, November 17, 1998.

86 Morris Nomi, "Violence Erupts as Ariel Sharon Visits
    Temple Mount," *Knight-Ridder News Service*, September
    28, 2000, 1.

86 "Rioting as Sharon Visits Islam Holy Site," *The Guardian*,
    September 29, 2000.

90 Charles M. Sennott, "Sharon Wins in a Landslide," *Boston
    Globe*, February 7, 2001, A1.

90 "Newsweek Interview: Ariel Sharon, Israeli Prime
    Minister, *Newsweek*, November 3, 2001, 23.

95 *Vital Speeches* 68, no. 13 (April 15, 2002): 387.

100 Simon Jeffery, "The Roadmap to Peace," *The Guardian
    Unlimited*, June 4, 2003, http://www.guardian.co.uk/
    theissues/article/0-6512.679445.00html (June 5, 2003).

101 Ariel Sharon interview, Israel Army Radio, May 7, 2003.

103 Emma Brockes, "The Bulldozer," *London Guardian*,
    November 7, 2001, 2.

SELECTED BIBLIOGRAPHY

Benziman, Uzi. *Sharon: An Israeli Caesar.* New York: Adama, 1985.

Dan, Uri. *Blood Libel.* New York: Simon and Schuster, 1987.

Finkelstein, Norman H. *Friends Indeed: The Special Relationship of Israel and the United States.* Brookfield, CT: Millbrook Press, 1989.

———. *Theodor Herzl: Architect of a Nation.* Minneapolis: Lerner Publications Company, 1991.

Miller, Anita, Jordan Miller, and Sigalit Zetouni. *Sharon: Israel's Warrior-Politician.* Chicago: Academy, 2002.

Sharon, Ariel, and David Chanoff. *Warrior: An Autobiography.* New York: Simon and Schuster, 1989.

Shavitt, Matti. *On the Wings of Eagles.* Tel Aviv: Olive Books, 1970.

FURTHER READING
AND WEBSITES

BOOKS

Cottrell, Robert C. *The Green Line: The Division of Palestine.* Philadelphia: Chelsea House, 2005.

Gilbert, Martin. *Atlas of the Arab-Israeli Conflict.* New York: Oxford University Press, 1993.

Goldstein, Margaret. *Israel in Pictures.* Minneapolis: Lerner Publications Company, 2004.

Greenfeld, Howard. *A Promise Fulfilled: Theodor Hertzl, Chaim Weitzmann, and David Ben-Gurion.* New York: Greenwillow, 2005.

Hayhurst, Chris. *Israel's War of Independence.* New York: Rosen, 2004.

Headlam, George. *Yasser Arafat.* Minneapolis: Lerner Publications Company, 2004.

Wagner, Heather Lehr. *Israel and the Arab World.* Philadelphia: Chelsea House, 2002.

WEBSITES

The Israeli Government: Ministry of Foreign Affairs
http://www.mfa.gov.il/mfa. This official site of the Israeli Ministry of Foreign Affairs offers general information about Israel and Ariel Sharon.

The Israeli Government: Prime Minister's Office
http://www.pmo.gov.il/PMOEng. This official website of the Israeli prime minister has links to speeches, current events, and news relating to Ariel Sharon and the Israeli government.

The Jerusalem Post
http://www.jpost.com. Read archived articles by and about Ariel Sharon and find current news about Israel.